The World of the
Bichon Frise

TS-245

Overleaf: 1995 Westminster Kennel Club Best of Breed winner *Ch. Chaminade Chamour Chances Are* owned by Barbara Stubbs, Lois Morrow, and Anita Carroll.

Distributed in the UNITED STATES to the Pet Trade by T.F.H. Publications, Inc., One T.F.H. Plaza, Neptune City, NJ 07753; distributed in the UNITED STATES to the Bookstore and Library Trade by National Book Network, Inc. 4720 Boston Way, Lanham MD 20706; in CANADA to the Pet Trade by H & L Pet Supplies Inc., 27 Kingston Crescent, Kitchener, Ontario N2B 2T6; Rolf C. Hagen Inc., 3225 Sartelon St. Laurent-Montreal Quebec H4R 1E8; in CANADA to the Book Trade by Vanwell Publishing Ltd., 1 Northrup Crescent, St. Catharines, Ontario L2M 6P5 ; in ENGLAND by T.F.H. Publications, PO Box 15, Waterlooville PO7 6BQ; in AUSTRA- LIA AND THE SOUTH PACIFIC by T.F.H. (Australia), Pty. Ltd., Box 149, Brookvale 2100 N.S.W., Australia; in NEW ZEALAND by Brooklands Aquarium Ltd. 5 McGiven Drive, New Plymouth, RD1 New Zealand; in Japan by T.F.H. Publications, Japan—Jiro Tsuda, 10-12-3 Ohjidai, Sakura, Chiba 285, Japan; in SOUTH AFRICA by Lopis (Pty) Ltd., P.O. Box 39127, Booysens, 2016, Johannesburg, South Africa. Published by T.F.H. Pub- lications, Inc.

MANUFACTURED IN THE
UNITED STATES OF AMERICA
BY T.F.H. PUBLICATIONS, INC.

The World of the
Bichon Frise

Ch. Beau Monde Miss Chaminade, by Mr. Beau Monde ex Parfait Apple Crunch, owned by Richard Beauchamp and Barbara Stubbs. Her championship was a final sentimental gesture to the great Mr. Beau Monde who was bred by Barbara and owned by Richard.

Anna Katherine Nicholas

Beautiful paintings of *Rivage D'Ami's Richochet Rogue* by the highly talented artist George Temmel, who grew up with the breed at his family's home on Long Island. A lovely little dog whose expression and beauty have been well captured by the artist.

Contents

ABOUT THE AUTHOR

Ch. Chaminade's Syncopation winning a Group 1st from the author. "Snidely Whiplash" was the first Best in Show winning Bichon Frise in the United States, having accomplished this achievement in May 1973. Owned by Mrs. William and shown by Ted Young, Jr.

Since early childhood, Anna Katherine Nicholas has been involved with dogs. Her first pets were a Boston Terrier, an Airedale, and a German Shepherd Dog. Then, in 1925, came the first of the Pekingese, a gfft from a friend who raised them. Now her home is shared with two Miniature Poodles and numerous Beagles.

Miss Nicholas is best known throughout the dog fancy as a writer and as a judge. Her first magazine article, published in Dog News magazine around 1930, was about Pekingese, and this was followed by a widely acclaimed breed column, "Peeking at the Pekingese," which appeared for at least two decades, originally in Dogdom, then, following the demise of that publication, in Popular Dogs. During the 1940s she was a Boxer columnist for PureBred Dogs/American Kennel Gazette and for Boxer Briefs. More recently many of her articles, geared to interest fanciers of every breed, have appeared in Pure-Bred Dogs/American Kennel Gazette, Show Dogs, Dog Fancy, .The World of the Working Dog. and for both the Canadian publications The Dog Fancier and Dogs in Canada. Her Dog World column, "Here, There and Everywhere," was the Dog Writers' Association of America winner of the Best Series in a Dog Magazine Award for 1979. Another feature article of hers, "Faster Is Not Better," published in Canine Chronicle, received Honorable Mention on another occasion. In 1970 Miss Nicholas won the Dog Writers' Association Award for the Best Technical Book of the Year with her Nicholas Guide to Dog Judging. In 1979 the revision of this book again

At the first specialty match of the Bichon Frise Club of America held in New York, on May 2nd 1971, Mrs. Helen D. Temmel wins the prestigious Bred-by-Exhibitor class with *Jeannine Chez Rivage d'Ami*. The judge is Anna Katherine Nicholas.

won this award, the first time ever that a revision had been so honored by this organization. Other important dog writer awards which Miss Nicholas has gained over the years have been the Gaines "Fido" and the Kennel Review "Winkles," these both on two occasions and each in the Dog Writer of the Year category.

It was during the 1930s that Miss Nicholas's first book, The Pekingese, appeared in print, published by the Judy Publishing Company. This book, and its second edition sold out quickly and is now a collector's item *The Skye Terrier Book*

which was published during the 1960s by the Skye Terrier Club of America.

During recent years, Miss Nicholas has been writing books consistently for T.F.H. These include *Successful Dog Show Exhibiting, The Book of the Rottweiler, The Book of the the Poodle, The Book of the Labrador Retriever, The Book of the English Springer Spaniel, The Book of the Golden Retriever, The Book of the German Shepherd Dog, The Book of the Shetland Sheepdog, The Book of the Miniature Schnauzer, The World of Doberman Pinschers, and The World of Rottweilers.* Plus, in another T.F.H.

series, *The Maltese, The Keeshond, The Chow Chow, The Poodle, The Boxer, The Beagle, The Basset Hound, The Dachshund (the latter three co-authored with Marcia A. Foy), The German Pointer, The Collie, The Weimaraner, The Great Dane, The Dalmatian, and numerous other titles. In the KW series she has done Rottweilers, Weimaraners, and Norwegian Elkhounds.*

Miss Nicholas's association with T.F.H. began in the early 1970s when she co-authored five books with Joan Brearley: *The Wonderful World of Beagles and Beagling* (also honored by the Dog Writers Association), *This is the Bichon Frise, The Book of the Pekingese, The Book of the Boxer, and This is the Skye Terrier.*

Miss Nicholas most recently has authored new books on some of the world's most recognizable dogs, included among these are *The Professional's Book of Rottweilers, The World of the Chinese Shar-Pei* and *The Staffordshire Terriers.*

Since 1934 Miss Nicholas has been a popular dog show judge, officiating at prestigious events throughout the United States and Canada. She is presently approved for all Hounds, all Terriers, all Toys and all Non-Sporting;

plus all Pointers, English and Gordon Setters, Vizslas, Weimaraners, and Wirehaired Pointing Griffons in the Sporting Group and Boxers and Dobermans in Working.

In 1970 she became only the third woman ever to have judged Best in Show at the famous Westminster Kennel Club event at Madison Square Garden in New York City, where she has officiated as well on some sixteen other occasions over the years. She has also officiated at such events as Santa Barbara, Chicago International, Morris and Essex, Trenton, Westchester, etc., in the United States; the Sportsman's and the Metropolitan among numerous others in Canada; and Specialty shows in several dozen breeds in both countries. She has judged in almost every one of the United States and in four of the Canadian Provinces. Her dislike of air travel has caused her to refrain from acceptance of constant invitations to officiate in other parts of the world.

In 1996 Miss Nicholas was awarded a Lifetime Achievement Award by Ken-L-Ration, one of the dog world's greatest honors.

Ch. Camelot's Brassy Nickel, CDX, a multiple Group, Specialty Show and all-breed Best in Show winner, taking a Group One placement under the author in 1984. Clifford Steel handling for Mrs. Pam Goldman, Livingston, New Jersey.

Origin of the Bichon

There are very few breeds of purebred dogs whose earliest history can be traced with absolute accuracy and certain confidence. This is highly understandable when one stops to consider that the centuries have been numerous and record-

We are told that many authorities considered Mme. Laisne of France to have been the best Bichon breeder of her day, breeding true Bichon type. Here are three of her dogs, *Sarah*, *Sidonie* and *Quetty*.

keeping of dogs was non-existent until very recently. We are left with bits and scraps of information; early artifacts, more often than not, leave the opinion in the eye of the beholder as far as the dogs are concerned. In this respect, the Bichon Frise has been among the easier breeds to place. The dogs have changed very little in appearance or character, and we have accepted the

idea that they were native to the Canary Islands. Now, after further research for this book, I am less certain. It seems more logical that rather than being *native* to the Canary Islands, the little white dogs were actually *developed* on the islands. It

seems that the sailors who went back and forth quite regularly between these islands and the Spanish mainland brought and left dogs on the island from which the Bichon Frise developed. My reason for this change in thinking is the fact that little dogs of Bichon type were very plentiful on the mainland and that the sailors made frequent trips back and forth with wares (including

Int. Ch. Jicky Des Closmyons was owned and bred by Mme. Laisne in France. Jicky was born in 1960 and widely admired for his super head and pigment.

little dogs) to sell or barter.

There are some who are of the opinion that the Canary Islands were named Canaria in honor of the multitude of dogs there, but if this is true, it could not have been the Bichon that populated the islands. This is because it was noted by King Juba of Mauretania, following his leading of an expedition to the islands, that the referred to dogs, at about 40 B.C., were described as "dogs of *great size*," which surely eliminates them from any part in the history of our completely different small curly Bichons.

Therefore there seems to be little question that the Bichons Frises have descended from the little mainland dogs, from whom they were *developed*, on the Canary Islands, and remained there reproducing themselves until the time came for their return to Europe. Everyone seems in complete agreement that the common ancestor of Bichons was the Barbet, a water spaniel credited with establishment of four categories, known collectively as the "Barbichon Group." These were the Bichon Bolognese, the Bichon Maltaise, the Bichon Ravenese, and the breed which concerns us here, the Bichon Frise. The latter enjoyed tremendous popularity in the Canary Islands, particularly on the largest of that group, Teneriffe Island, in honor of which this little dog he became the Bichon Teneriffe, and remained as such until the 1930s.

Throughout the Renaissance period the Bichon took on immediately. The world of style and fashion loved them and they were seen in Europe at many social gatherings serving as accessories. Carried tucked under an arm by the most stylish ladies, the little dogs softened the appearance of the severely plain dresses that were fashionable at that point in time. The bright, inquisitive

small dog beautifully groomed was a most desired and coveted companion to the best-dressed ladies.

This was the period when the dogs were clipped to a leonine appearance known as the "lion clip," which was considered chic and amusing by their owners. They did look adorable, and attracted many new fans and admirers with their "miniature lion" appearance.

One famous lady who loved the Bichon Frise was Cleopatra, Queen of the Nile, who not only admired the little dogs but is said to have owned several of them.

Members of the majority of the royal families seem always to be and to have been animal lovers. In the case of the Bichon Teneriffe, they quickly added Francis I to their fans during his reign (1515-1547). Not to mention the heights of popularity that were attained when everyone was anxious to emulate the devotion of Henry III (1574-1589). Henry kept his pets constantly with him by carrying them in a tray-like basket tied by ribbons around his neck. These favorite darlings of the court were groomed, powdered and perfumed in

A beautiful headstudy of Ch. *Stardom's Niki de Staramour, ROM* who is owned by Mrs. Celeste Fleishman. This famous picture appeared in the *Philadelphia Evening Bulletin* on November 5, 1972.

Ch. Stardom's Niki de Staramour, ROM is by Ch. Titan de Wanarbry (France) ex Jean Rank's Crystal. Along with his sire, "Niki" remained in the top-ten winning Bichons for several consecutive years. Owner, Mrs. Celeste Fleishman, Staramour Bichons, Gwynedd Valley, Pennsylvania.

a manner attesting to the importance of their position in the Royal household.

So carefully were these little dogs groomed and immaculately maintained that the French verb "bichon," which translates "to pamper, to curl, to make beautiful," was created in their honor. The reign of Napoleon III was another triumphant period for Bichons. This spanned the period of 1852-1870, with the small white "furries" adding to their popularity and fame.

But fame is, to say the least, fickle. And so it was not too unusual that suddenly, after a lengthy period of adulation for Bichons among the gentry, the breed went out of style. To some breeds and types of dog this might have proven catastrophic. But not so in the case of these merry, "people-loving" little dogs, with their gaiety of spirit and ideal dispositions. They were endowed with too many assets not to make out well, although in different circles than before. Although the change in their appearance was from perfectly groomed to shaggy, they made their

Ch. Chaminade's Syncopation became the first Bichon to win an all-breed Best in Show in the United States to the delight of his owner Mrs. William Tabler of Long Island and his handler Ted Young, Jr. "Snidely" literally swept through eastern show rings like a storm, becoming #3 Non-Sporting Dog in 1973 and #6 Non-Sporting Dog in 1974.

way into a long line of hearts, and earned their living well, as street dogs. Now they were referred to as "the little sheepdog" due to their shaggy, unkempt appearance. They stepped quickly into the role of clown and entertainer, for which they were well fitted, being of high intelligence, bright and eager to learn. One saw Bichons trotting happily alongside organ grinders, for whose audience they displayed assorted tricks and friendly good humor. Their talents as entertainers included perfection of amazingly intricate routines, keeping them well in demand for that purpose. Few indeed were the fairs or circuses that did not include a dog act performed by the Bichons!

But just to watch and make friends with the little dogs as they cavorted gaily on the streets with the organ grinder was amusement in itself, as the little dogs' zest for life, sense of humor, and complete friendliness made them popular with, as they say, "children of all ages."

This was the period during which the Bichon had "fallen upon bad times." Yet, thinking about it, one cannot fail to wonder if possibly the merry little dogs were actually happier than they had been as the perfumed, well groomed, pampered pets of the rich and famous.

Soldiers stationed in Europe of course noticed, and were attracted to, these outgoing small canines. We understand that a number of them were brought home by members of the armed forces as hostilities ended, but only as pets since formal breeding of them at that time was non-existent. As was their custom, they fared well in their new surroundings, continuing to attract friends by their personality. Still today I recall one that belonged to a lady who worked for us when I was a child that I since have realized had to have been a Bichon Frise. In those days, however, he

was just a cute little dog with whom I enjoyed playing.

EUROPEAN BICHONS COME OF AGE

It was during the early 1930s that everything seemed to come together for the little dogs, then known as Bichons Teneriffes. The Societe Central Canine de France adopted an official standard for them on March 5, 1933. The standard was prepared with diligence and care by noted breeder Mme. Adabie, whose Steren Vor Kennels in France were already well esteemed on the Continent and whose dogs provided foundation stock in the United States and elsewhere. Discussion arose regarding the naming of the breed, the feeling having been that Bichon

Teneriffe was no longer suitable since so much time elapsed since the dogs had departed from there. Considerable discussion regarding the possible new names followed, with everyone seeming at odds on a final decision. Finally, that highly esteemed lady, Mme. Nizet de Leemans,

Above: *Ch. Lola des Closmyons* owned and bred by Mme. Laisne in France. An important dog of the early 1960s in France. Left: *Ch. Chateau's Idealbo Rivage d'Ami, CDX*, born in December 1968, was the first male Bichon to earn a CD title. "Bo" was owned by Mrs. Helen Temmel, of Dunedin, Florida, who purchased him from breeder, Millicent Cole.

for many years president of the International Canine Federation (the F.C.I. as we think of it today), came up with the thought that a descriptive name should be chosen, for which she suggested Bichon a Poil Frise, which translates "Bichon of the Curly Coat." That evidently received the approval of all concerned as the name promptly was

dogs in Europe came to a halt. But after the ravages of war had ended, people resumed their normal lives and once more attention was paid to the Bichon a Poil Frise, but now with a new dimension. In addition to bringing pleasure as a family pet and companion, the postwar Bichon was destined to gain

Cali-Col's Shalimar, bred and owned by pioneer breeder Mrs. Gertrude Fournier, winning the Brood Bitch Class at the very first "B" Match Show for Bichons ever held in the United States on August 4, 1974 at San Diego, California. Dr. Sam Draper is the judge making the award.

adopted.

The Bichon a Poil Frise was admitted to the stud book of the French Kennel Club on October 18, 1934, as a "French-Belgian breed."

The future for the breed was looking bright until the onset of World War II, when again the breeding of

prominence in a new field: that of a successful show dog.

France and Belgium have long been closely associated with the progress of the Bichon, where many outstanding members of the breed first saw the light of day. Two highly esteemed specialty clubs are the French *Club des Bichons* and the Belgian Club *Belge du Bichon.* From the earliest breeding programs on, records and pedigrees have been kept with utmost care, and an excellent base formed for the continued development of the breed.

In the early days following official recognition of the Bichon a Poil Frise, there was not a wide gene pool with which breeders could work. Thus, rather tight line-breeding took place, perhaps for the better. One had little choice other than this type of breeding, which over the years has become generally acknowledged as the most successful route to recreating type and quality.

There have been some notably admired and highly successful breeders to whom tribute is due for producing outstanding Bichons, both at home and abroad. The very first Bichon with whom I became closely acquainted was Quilet des Frimousettes, who had been imported by a close friend of mine, Mrs. N. Clarkson Earl, Jr., of Ridgefield, CT. Bred in France, he came to America to help a new breeder of Bichons start off properly. Sadly, the death of this lady's husband caused a change of plans and the dispersal of her entire kennel, including the Skye Terriers and Silkys for which she was famous. Quilet sired champion Bichons Frises here and was widely admired by all who knew him. The owner of Frimousette Bichons is Mlle. J. Miligari.

Mme. Suzanne Mazeas Nicolas has achieved success with her Wanabry Bichons. Her fine dogs figure prominently in the pedigrees of many famed and correct individuals.

Several of Mme. E. Laisne's peers describe her as "quite possibly the best

Photographed circa 1970, this is Staramour Sir Dandy by La Jolie Bibi de Reenroy ex Spunkie le Tresor de Reenroy.

BEST OF
OPPOSITE SEX
PHOTO BY *Graham*

Above: *Ch. Jalwin Illumine de Noel, ROM* was one of Ann Hearn's early bitches. A daughter of Ch. Cali-Col's Ulysses ex Ch. Cherokee Candy De Noel, she was bred by Virginia Haley. Right: Puppies bred by Richard Beauchamp are *Ch. Beau Monde The Actor* and *Ch. Beau Monde The Author.*

breeder of Bichons in France."

Mlle. Maynieu owns the Bourbiel Kennels, another of note.

As I study photographs of her dogs, I have acquired deep admiration for Mme.

C. DeFarge and her "la Buthieres." They are correctly true to type and a credit to the breed.

Another fine French kennel, Steren Vor, owned by Mme. Abadie, furnished important early breeding stock when the breed was developing in the United States. Belgium was right up front alongside of France where development of the Bichon Frise is concerned. The Milton Kennels, owned by M. and Mme. A. Bellotte, were among the foremost. Their dogs were used frequently for breeding, and are to be noted in many early pedigrees.

The former wife of Albert Baras, Mme. Baras-Berben of Belgium, owns de la Persaliere Kennels, a name closely associated with famous Bichons of the

Shelby Roberts, daughter of Ellen and David Roberts, with her favorite Bichon, "Peaches."

Right: From the early 1970s *Ch. Chaminade's Syncopation,* owned by Mrs. W.B. Tabler, was America's first consistent Best in Show winner.

earlier days. Albert Baras owned numerous outstanding dogs, gained fame as a judge, and was an important early member of the Club Belge du Bichon, serving as its president. His enthusiasm and interest in the breed endeared him to the Americans, among whom he had a wide circle of friends.

Right: *Ch. Reenroy's Ami du Kilkanny,* by Dapper Dan de Gascoigne ex Little Nell of Cali-Col. Owned by Barbara Stubbs.

Am., Danish, Int. Ch. Beau Monde Cameo Callboy is owned by and adding to the success of Chouan Kennels, G. Hyman and H. Rusk, Denmark.

Bichons in the United States

The American history of the Bichon Frise dates back to 1956 when Mr. and Mrs. Francois Picault (Francois and Helene) arrived in America having emigrated from Dieppe, France. They brought with them their original two Bichons, Eddy White de Steren Vor and Etoile de Steren Vor, both of whom had been purchased from the Steren Vor Kennels made famous by Mme. Adabie in France. So excited were the Picaults over the Bichons that they decided almost immediately to become breeders of these little dogs. They selected the kennel identification "de La Hoop," which they then registered with the French Kennel Club. Etoile, bred to Eddy White, produced her first litter the following year, consisting of five puppies. The enthusiasm of the Picaults was obviously growing by leaps and bounds through all of this, and during 1956 they sent for and imported two additional bitches, Gypsie de Wanabry (representing Mme. Suzanne Mazeas-Nicolas's Bichons in France) and Gavotte de Hoop. These four importations and the five Eddy White-Etoile puppies formed the nucleus from which our modern Bichon has emerged here in the United States.

The Picaults had made the move from France to the United States for two purposes. The first was the fact that their daughter, Rene Dahl, moved to and settled in Milwaukee. The second was, at the urge of Mme. Adabie, an effort to introduce the Bichons to the United States, which they looked upon as a promising means of income. Mr. Picault unfortunately died of a heart attack during January of 1972, just as the breed was on the threshold of AKC recognition.

It was in 1957 that the Picaults became acquainted with Mrs. Azalea Gascoigne, whose interest had been attracted by the Bichons. Mrs. Gascoigne purchased Hermine de Hoop (from the original Eddy White-Etoile litter) from the Picaults in 1958, and bred her to Jou Jou de Hoop for a litter that included Andre and April de Gascoigne.

Mrs. Gascoigne travelled to France in 1962, during which a highlight was her

attendance at the Paris dog show. Three lovely bitches accompanied her on her return home, purchased from Mme. Miligari of the Frimousettes. One of this trio, Lady des Frimousettes, was bred to Andre de Gascoigne (Hermine-Jou Jou son). She took her place in American Bichon history as this litter produced the very important "pillar of the breed"—Mexican Ch. Dapper Dan De Gascoigne, whose success and dominance as a sire are a matter of record. In those days Mexico was the only

part of North America where a Bichon could gain championship honors; thus Dapper Dan's achievement in this respect brought joy to the Bichon fraternity. Duffy De Gascoigne was also from this litter and became a consistent winner for Dr. Irving Kohn back in the early match show days.

In Joan Brearley's and my book *This is the Bichon Frise*, also a T.F.H. publication, we printed, with permission, some extremely interesting comments on the early dogs made by the eminent authority Mrs. Gertrude

Mrs. Ellen Iverson MacNeille holds her famous winning Bichon, *Ch. Hillwood Brass Band* as handler, Ted Young, Jr., holds the ribbon. Brass Band was a multiple Best in Show and Group winner with rating among the top ten Non-Sporting dogs during the early 1980s.

Ch. Beau Monde The Iceman did some notable winning for Dr. and Mrs. Anthony DiNardo of Hartford, Connecticut during the late 1960s and 1970s under Jane Kamp Forsyth's handling.

Fournier of the world famous Cali-Col Kennels, for an article in the Bichon Frise Club of America publication, *Bichon Tales.* Mrs. Fournier had long been a successful breeder/exhibitor of Collies when she first saw the Bichon Frise and promptly succumbed to its charms. Mrs. Fournier met the Picaults after they had moved from Milwaukee to San Diego and when they had come to realize that the Bichons were *not* (at least not yet) catching the public's interest as they had anticipated when leaving France. To the contrary, enthusiasm was at a low ebb despite the breed's natural charms. The American fanciers were obviously not overcome with a desire to purchase or own an expensive dog not yet accepted for registration and recognition by the American Kennel Club. This had left the Picaults sorely disappointed as their dreams of instant popularity for the breed vanished. Mrs. Fournier learned of all this from friends, so being interested, and herself a San Diego resident, she made an appointment to go to see the dogs for herself.

The upshot of all this was that eventually Mrs. Fournier took over the Picaults' Bichons. With some further additions of her own, she established the Cali-Cols, who have provided the foundation stock for many other highly successful and famous kennels.

In reading Mrs. Fournier's words on the subject we have learned that Eddy White, who gained 17 Championship wins in France, was very small, carried tremendous coat, and had color on his ears and body. Etoile, on the other hand, was slightly larger; completely white with a loosely curled heavy coat. Gypsie was approximately 10½ inches high at the withers, had color on body and ears, was slightly cobbier than the others, and excelled in front and hindquarters. No description of Gavotte de Hoop is included, but comment is made on a very petite Gigolo, and on Gigi de Hoop at the other extreme, measuring all of 14 inches and carrying a woolly coat. Gigi was a daughter of Eddy White and Etoile. Noting the wide deviation in type of these closely related Bichons, one realizes that the breeders over the early years really had their work cut out for them. It is no wonder that many of the early dogs shown were noticeably

Legacy's Candy de la Garre, owner-handled by Dorothy Siebert, winning Best Puppy at the Bichon Frise Club of America National Specialty on May 15, 1980 in San Diego, California. The judge is Dr. Samuel Draper, and Mrs. Gertrude Fournier of Cali-Col fame is presenting the trophy.

dissimilar in balance, size, and coat texture, among other features.

The great Mexican Ch. Dapper Dan de Gascoigne accompanied Mrs. Gascoigne on a trip to California in 1964. He was such a tremendous contribution to the future of the breed that Mrs. Gascoigne allowed this superlative dog to remain in California with Mrs. Fournier! Later he went to Mrs. Mayree Butler, who was another of the important people responsible for the Bichon as we know the breed today. Dapper Dan sired an impressive number of dogs destined to favorably influence the breed in the U.S. and many other countries, creating a number of top producing lines among his offspring and descendants.

The name "Chaminade," which identifies the Bichons Frises of Mrs. Barbara Stubbs, is undoubtedly the best known in the Bichon world. I seriously doubt that there is a Bichon-conscious person anywhere who is unaware of Mrs. Stubbs, the Chaminade dogs, and their important influence as the breed has developed. Barbara has been involved ever since the first members of the breed arrived in California, and remains so today as a breeder and exhibitor. She recently joined in partnership with Mrs. Lois

Ch. Alpenglow Ashley du Chamour, by Ch. Cragdale's Saluto du Chamour ex Ch. Chaminade Blue Velvet, was the #1 Non-Sporting Dog in the United States in 1988. His wins include 12 Bests in Show and 71 Group One placements. Owned by Lois Morrow, "Ashley" was bred by Linda Day and Barbara Stubbs.

Ch. Reenroy's Ami du Kilkanny, by Dapper Dan de Gascoigne ex Little Nell of Cali-Col, and *Petit Galant de St. George,* by Monsieur Mieux du Pic Four ex Cali-Col's Nugget. These two were the foundation of the famed Chaminade lines which are owned by Barbara Stubbs in La Jolla, California. "Ami" is the dam of the Top Producing sire of the breed, Ch. Chaminade Mr. Beau Monde.

Morrow, whose dogs are identified by the Chamour kennel name.

Like Gertrude Fournier and Mayree Butler, Barbara Stubbs is a Californian (La Jolla in her case). I think we might almost say that our Bichons were developed in California, as the principal work and breeding for the foundation and stabilization of the breed actually took place there, although the effects have been felt around the world. After all, the early Milwaukee contingent "went West" and the others who got Bichons rolling were already Californians! Thus much of what set the breed on the right course took place there with, of course, interest spreading to the other areas of the States as soon as fanciers started to realize what they were missing.

It was in 1966 that Barbara Stubbs laid the foundation for Chaminade with the acquisition of three who proved to be great ones. Ch. Cali-Col's Robespierre, producer of 14 champions; Ch. Reenroy's Ami du Kilkanny, producer of five champions; and Petit Galant de St. George, sire of ten champions. This trio was selected by Barbara on which to found her kennel and strain. As one looks at the record, these choices could hardly have been improved upon.

Robespierre was the sire selected to whom Ami

Top: *Ch. Chaminade Le Blanc Chamour* was a 1989 Pedigree Award Winner for Lois Morrow and Richard and Carolyn Vida. His breeders are Lois Morrow, Barbara Stubbs and G. and N. Harrell. He is a son of Ch. Craigdale's Ole' Rondi and he is the sire of the top winning Ch. Chaminade Larkshire Lafitte who has gained a formidable array of all breed and specialty Best in Show awards. These three Bichons are representative of the finest in conformation and in bloodlines. Bottom: *Ch.Chaminade Chamaur Diva* belongs to Laurie Bender of Los Angeles, California. Photo courtesy of Barbara Stubbs

Ch. Chaleen's Lockiel Chaminade, by Ch. Chaminade Le Jazz Hot ex Ch. Alpenglow du Chamour, carries on the lovely type and beauty of this line. Breeder/owners are Anita Carroll, Lois Morrow and Barbara Stubbs. Handled by Wood Wornal.

should be bred. An inspired combination from which came Richard Beauchamp's wonderful dog, Ch. Chaminade Mr. Beau Monde. With 69 champions eventually sired by Mr. Beau Monde, he became, and even after all these years remains, the all-time top-producing sire among Bichons.

Mr. Beau Monde's litter sister, Ch. Chaminade's Sonata, was bred to Petit Galant. Again another inspired choice as this gave the United States its very first Bichon ever to win Best in Show at an AKC championship event, Ch. Chaminade Syncopation. Better known as "Snidely Whiplash," he introduced Bichons to the dog show general public by making all who saw him want to own a Bichon immediately. That historic first Best in Show soon grew to seven Bests in Show plus 60 Group One Placements, handled by Ted Young, Jr. for Mrs. William Tabler of

The wonderful *Ch. Chaminade Mr. Beau Monde* pictured finishing his championship at Golden Gate Kennel Club in January 1974. Owned by Richard Beauchamp, Mr. Beau Monde was handled to his show success by Joe Waterman. Sired by Ch. Cali-Col's Robspierre ex Ch. Reenroy Ami du Kilkanny, this dog became a Top Producing Bichon Frise with 65 champions to his credit.

America's first Best in Show winning Bichon Frise, *Ch. Chaminade Syncopation*, owned by Mrs. William Tabler, and his handler, Ted Young, Jr. Photo courtesy of Ellen and David Roberts.

New York. He contributed well as a sire along with his show successes, his champion progeny numbering 14.

Richard Beauchamp has been deeply involved with the Bichon since its early days in the United States. He acquired Ch. Chaminade's Mr. Beau Monde in 1971, after some years of association with the Bichon world. As owner and editor of *Kennel Review* magazine, Richard is somewhat of a world traveler, which has proven beneficial to Bichons in many different parts of the world where Richard is known and respected for his wide knowledge of dogs. It stands to reason that Mr. Beau Monde's sons and daughters and their

Ch. Pillow Talk's Special K handled by David Roberts to Group One Placement at Merrimack Valley Kennel Club in May, 1992. Breeders/owners, Tracy and Lori Kornfeld, Ridgefield, Connecticut.

kennels. One notes the significance of this as we study the backgrounds of highly successful bloodlines from Australia, New Zealand, Great Britain, South Africa, South America, parts of Europe, etc. Richard in his own kennel has bred more than 50 champion Bichons.

The breeders we have mentioned in this chapter really set the stage for what would follow as others became interested and involved with this breed. Cali-Col, Reenroy, Chaminade and Beau Monde, with the early French and Belgian importations of de Hoop and de Gascoigne, created a dog designed for success. Now breeders throughout the United States are working

progeny over the years have been in demand from around the world for the foundation or enhancement of breeding programs in Bichon

Ch. Beau Monde Yankee Clipper one of the outstanding Bichons bred by Richard Beauchamp and Pauline Waterman.

diligently to continue using to full advantage the quality background to enhance their own lives.

We owe a tremendous debt to the early breeders for whom it could not have been easy. There were too many deviations in type to be stabilized, and other problems had to be worked out. But they took it all in stride. What a satisfaction it must be now to these people and to the many others who joined the Bichon fancy to note the excellence we are seeing in our show rings, the standardization of type which has been accomplished, and the success and beauty of the little dogs!

Dozens of other breeders have played and are playing exciting roles in the success of their beloved breed as you will note throughout the pages of this book. All the more remarkable when one considers that the breed has only been recognized here for about two decades!

Interest spread rapidly from the Pacific Coast eastward, with much activity in between as well. Now dozens of people are breeding excellent Bichons and enjoying every moment of it. It was not long before AKC recognition that the Bichons Frises in America received a great and valued compliment from Mme. Nizet de Leemans, the famous lady who had judged throughout the world and was at the time President of the Standards Committee for the Federation Canine de International (the F.C.I.). During a 1971 visit to the United States, she stated that, in her opinion, the "American Bichons have become better than those in France and Belgium." Warm praise indeed from so renowned and respected an authority whose interest in Bichons had already been over a period of several decades!

The wider ownership and increased popularity of Bichons in the United States quickly reached a point where there was need of a specialty club to

provide a learning base and other activities for those interested in the breed. Also a registry for Bichons was needed for their application to become an AKC recognized breed. A breed standard suitable for presentation was also high on the list of priorities.

Optimism was high for the success of the breed throughout the 1960s. More fanciers were

Ch. Sundance Glen Elfred Cheri Amor owned by Terry and Dennis Alabrande of Selden, New York completing title at Riverhead in March 1992.

becoming aware of the many assets of these little dogs, and, as they were seen with greater frequency, curiosity about them and a thought of owning one became expressed more frequently by dog lovers. Not the mad enthusiasm with which some had hoped the breed would be greeted, but a steady-growing awareness that this, indeed, was a dog to cherish and enjoy.

Thus it was during May, 1964 that a group of 28 people, all of whom became members, met for the purpose of discussing and organizing what would become the Bichon Frise Club of America. These members at that time represented only four states. A previous effort had been made back in Milwaukee, but that had fizzled into more of a social club than one devoted to the best interests of a breed of dog. This time it would be different, as the breeders were becoming more cognisant of how the promotion of such a group should be handled, and it *was* with a steady even rate of growth and interest.

Officers elected at this first meeting were Mrs. Azalea Gascoigne as President and Mrs. Gertrude Fournier as the first Registrar. Mayree Butler and Goldy Olsen were also among those involved in the founding of the club, with Mrs. Butler in 1967 becoming President.

Within the first 19 months of the BFCA's existence (1964-65), 34 litters were registered by the club and 133 individual Bichons. Of these earliest registrations, eight individuals had been imported from France, registered by the French Kennel Club, and three were from Belgium, registered with their kennel club. By 1966, a noticeable growth pattern was taking shape. The original 28 members had grown in numbers to 90, with 300 individual Bichons registered during that period.

Still greater growth was recorded for the following two years, with 1968 seeing the membership rise to 200 persons from 37 states, the District of Columbia, and Canada (the latter for the purpose of using the BFCA Registry to register Canadian litters and individual dogs temporarily as Canada did not have a club registry at that time). By January 1970 the membership of the Bichon Frise Club of America was standing at the very respectable total of 350 fanciers from 38 states (including Alaska and

Ch. Chaminade Phoenicia, by Petit Galant de St. George ex C'Est Bon de Pigalle was the first Bichon bitch to ever win the Non-Sporting Group in the United States. Owned and shown by Teena Sarkissian Runyan and Marie Sarkissian.

Ch. Jalwin Panache of Win Mar, ROMX was one of the all-time top producing Bichon bitches with 14 champions to her credit. Among her very beautiful progeny is Ch. Jalwin Just A Jiffy, BIS, BISS, and multiple Group winner.

Hawaii), 408 litters, and 1040 individual Bichons registered. An exciting note on which to begin that very important part of Bichon history, the decade of the 1970s. It was on September 1, 1970 that the Bichon Frise was accepted into the Miscellaneous Class at AKC dog shows. Now they were really rolling with better things coming closer. Bichons were admitted to the AKC stud book registry in October, 1972, and they were approved to become members of the Non-Sporting Group on April 4, 1973.

As I am certain we are all aware, almost everywhere in the world the Bichon Frise has been and remains classified as a *Toy* dog. Many feel they actually are not, at least by modern standards. It had obviously been the original intention of the AKC to classify them as Toys here, too. But the

Bichon fancy worked very hard to persuade them that these dogs as we see them today are larger and more heavily boned than any of the Toy breeds; thus they would look out of place competing as something they actually are not. To everyone's relief the American Kennel Club listened, considered and decided that the USA had made their point. So the Bichons, at least in this country, are in their proper classification.

The first Bichon Frise to be registered with the AKC was Sha-Bob's Nice Girl Missy. She gained her championship and is to be found in the pedigrees of some noted dogs today.

The Bichon Frise Club of America has been joined over the years by numerous hardworking and extremely valuable affiliated clubs. They do a splendid job in support of the breed and carry an interesting and useful schedule of events for their members each year. The first of the affiliates was the Bichon Frise Club of San Diego, which also held the first match show for Bichons during 1963, drawing an entry of 12 Bichons to the Hotel del Coronado. Included in the entry was Eddy White de Steren Vor. The officiating judge was Lee Schaller.

Meanwhile, a strong group of interested fanciers back East had been busy at work popularizing the Bichon, circulating information about them, and gathering their forces to take a major step for the benefit of this beautiful breed with which many were just becoming enamored. This resulted in the formation of the second affiliate club to become active, the Greater New York Bichon Frise Fanciers, which organized officially in 1968. It is notable that within a period of only two years these folks had maintained so busy a schedule that they had already held four highly successful match shows prior to 1971, when they hosted the very first National Specialty! The entire Eastern dog show world was in high gear over the anticipated viewing of the Bichons, which was to take place in a popular New York City midtown hotel. When the great day rolled around, the ballroom was packed to capacity with Bichons, Bichon owners from all parts of the United States, and a star-studded galaxy of

Ch. Chaminade Larkshire Lafitte, owned by Lois Morrow who co-bred him with J.O'Dea and Barbara Stubbs, has amassed an amazing number of Bests in Show, Variety Groups and other prestigious wins under Bill McFadden's handling.

Ch. D'Shar's Rendezvous du Chamour, by Cameo Chaminade Chant ex Ch. Bryamar Capice du Chaminade, is pictured here with his owner Lois Morrow. This double Tempo grandson was a top winner in 1982 and a top producer of 15 champions. The most notable of these latter being Ch. Craigdale's Olé Rhondi.

prominent dog authorities anxious to see this historic happening.

Having been the judge for that specialty, and officiated in the breed with frequency from then till now, this show still remains in my mind as one of my most memorable judging assignments. The entry, for the first time in the breed, ran more than 100 dogs, some of them almost unbelievably beautiful. The top dogs from the leading kennels of that period were all that I had anticipated even by present standards and I feel that my winners that day could still take top honors on many occasions. Since then there have been changes (improvements) in the standard and excellent

progress on the part of the breeders where quality of the dogs is concerned. On thinking back over the dogs and bitches of that event, one can easily understand the tremendous quality they brought to future generations. The descendants of those Bichons still carry the banner in the breed today, for they included the great Mexican Ch. Cali-Col's Shadrach (Best Adult) and the memorable *Reenroy's* Riot Act, who was early in her career and won Best Puppy.

The Bichon Frise Club of America held the next exciting Bichon Show "happening." This one was the first Sanction B match for the breed, hosted by the Bichon Frise Club of San Diego on April 7, 1973, the very first weekend following the Bichon's entry into AKC point competition. Tom Stevenson judged 111 Bichons there at the Flamingo Hotel in Las Vegas in a never-to-be-forgotten occasion for those attending.

The first licensed point specialty show of the Bichon Frise Club of America was held in May, 1976 at San Diego. Since then the location for the Nationals is on a rotating basis, with them being "hosted" by the affiliated

local clubs through what now has grown to a week-long festivity.

Local specialty clubs for the Bichon Frise in the United States now include a dozen or more situated in Texas (both Dallas and Houston), California (Greater Los Angeles, San Diego, and Northern California), Northern New Jersey, Puget Sound, Southern New England, Chicagoland, Greater New York, Greater St. Louis, and Southeastern Michigan. Those seeking further information regarding communication with these clubs should do so either through the breeder of your dog or the corresponding secretary of the Bichon Frise Club of America, whose name and address is available through the American Kennel Club, 51 Madison Avenue, New York, N.Y., 10011. Specialty club officials often change, but the AKC will have the current officials of the national club on file, so they can put you in touch without delay.

The Bichon Frise competed in the Miscellaneous Class for only a relatively short period, from September, 1971 until April, 1973. During this period, the Bichon people energetically supported these classes

and there are some dogs from there whom we feel deserve inclusion in this book. For example, the world-famous Int., Dutch, French and German Ch. Tarzan de la Persaliere, who entered his first show at age 9 $^1/_2$ months on October 25, 1970. Tarzan became Top Bichon under the Rothman System in *Popular Dogs Magazine* and won a Best Puppy in Show award. In 1972 Tarzan was sent to Belgium, where he was shown to many honors by Mrs. Albert Baras. To my knowledge he did not return to the U.S. but he certainly had considerable impact on Bichon fanciers here.

Then there was William's Snow Princess of Rank belonging to Robert W. Koeppel, who remains active today in the Bichon

Ch. C. and D.'s Samson, by Ch. C. and D.'s King of the Road ex Ch. C. and D.'s Bewitching Summer, is a champion of the mid-1980s handled by Carol Millar for owner Nancy Schmidt, Oshkosh, Wisconsin.

Ch. C. and D.'s Distan Lace and Promise interestingly was sired by the Japanese import Am. Ch. C. and D.'s Taro The Great ex Ch. C and D.'s Bunnyrun Full Tilt. Owned by Nancy C. Schmidt, Oshkosh, Wisconsin, for whom Carol Millar is the handler.

world and is a consistent exhibitor of some handsome and outstanding dogs. Gertrude Fournier's Cali-Col's Shadrach was in there and gained a good show record under Michael Dougherty's handling, as was Reenroy's Ami du Kilkenny, one of her foundation bitches representing Barbara Stubbs.

Bichon folks were very wholehearted in their support of the Miscellaneous Classes, all with a singleness of purpose aimed at full classification for the breed as fast as possible. *Popular Dogs Magazine* carried a point rating system compiled by Martin Rothman, who was closely associated with the Bichon world in the East. The Rothmans had outstanding

stock in their kennel and were among the hardest workers for the cause in the Long Island area. As was Estelle Kellerman and her daughter, Wendy.

Delores and Charles Wolske, C and D Bichons, were already active then and remained so for years. Helen Temmel, then of Long Island, now of Florida, was very much into Bichon obedience and showing in conformation and highly successful in both fields. There is Stella G. Raabe, owner of the well-known Stardom's Odin Rex, Jr., found in so many important pedigrees in the U.S. and abroad. Henry Furst was an early President of the Bichon Frise Club of Greater New York who is now living in Florida and still enjoying Bichons. I must also acknowledge Melvin and Marvel Brown, Mel Mar's Bichons in Michigan, as well as Bonnie Caison, owner of Frosty Boy Tico. And so very many more who helped to shape the destinies of the Bichons of today!

The Bichon Frise as a member of the Non-Sporting Group wasted no time at all in making his presence felt. He hit the jackpot almost immediately. Soon, one after another of these charmers was bringing home leading honors at a steady rate.

Remember, please, as you think about this, that was in the days when some of the world's greatest Poodles were very much into competition; not to mention those superior Keeshonden on the Pacific coast, some great Dalmatians and Chow Chows, and some extraordinary Boston Terriers and Bulldogs. But being the "new kid on the block" hardly caused the Bichons or their owners a moment's concern. They were ready to go—and they went—right clear to the top.

Although the breed was not admitted to competition as a Non-Sporting Dog until April of 1973, success did not keep the breed waiting! By the close of that year, Ch. Chaminade's Syncopation had become the first Best in Show Bichon in the United States and Ch. Cali-Col's Scalawag was close on his heels as the second. Syncopation took four Best in Show awards for Mrs. William Tabler. Scalawag made off with two for Mrs. G. Pillsbury. Both of these American-bred dogs contributed enormously to the quality and prestige of American Bichons, and represented the most hard working and admired fanciers of that period. During that same year prestigious awards in the form of first in the Non-Sporting Group went to Ch.

C and D's Kount Christopher, owned by the well known and successful breeders, C. and D. Wolske. Ch. Reenroy's Ritzie Doll gained half a dozen.

Looking back in time to 1975, we note only one Best in Show that year went to a Bichon—Ee's R Encore owned by P. Klinkhardt. Syncopation, Scalawag, and Lois Morrow's Ch. Chaminade's Tempo all won and placed in numerous Groups, as did Ch. Keystone Christine owned by Mrs. G. Slocum.

On to 1976 and two Bests in Show, 11 Group Firsts and other placements to Ch. C and D's Beau Monde Blizzard, owned by Doberman breeders Dr. and Mrs. Anthony Di Nardo. Another Best in Show winner that year was Ch. Jadeles the Kid H H Pride,

Ch. C. and D.'s Amanda Rae is a new champion owned by Nancy Schmidt, Oshkosh, Wisconsin.

Top: *Ch.
Crockery
Beau Monde
Eclipse* is
owned by
Nancy
Shapland.

who additionally gained nine Groups and 11 placements for owner N. Makowiec. Also in 1976, Nancy Shapland won an impressive number of awards, including 35 Group placements with her Ch. C and D's Stargazer, which was an exciting forecast of things to come.

Lots of Groups for Bichons during 1977, and some new names on the list of winners. Ch. Vogelflight's Music Man led the breed that year by winning Best in Show, 21 Group firsts, and an impressive 53 Group placements for owners Mr. and Mrs. B. Busk. Tempo, now co-owned by Lois Morrow and Phyllis Tabler, gained nine Group Firsts and 23 placements. Ch. Kobold's Kilimanjaro five Groups and 32 placements for S. Fry. And Ch. Paw Paw Knickerbocker won several Group firsts and 32 placements for Mr. Koeppel.

Ch. Jadeles the Kid H H Pride also made a good showing for N. Makowiec.

In 1978 Bichons were really rolling along. Music Man took three Bests in Show, 46 Group firsts, 35 Group placements, and was number three Non-Sporting Dog. The Iceman had a Best in Show, 14 Group firsts and 36 placements. Kilimanjaro had 11 Groups, 36 placements. Ch. Beau Monde Regal Rose won six Groups and 17 placements; and Ch. Norvic's Easy Does It, two Groups, 19 placements for R. and L. Kendal.

Ellen Iverson had the number nine Non-Sporting Dog in 1979 in Ch. Vogelflight's Choir Master, who won two Bests in Show and seven Groups with 25 Group placements. Vogelflight's Music Man also had two Bests along with 12 Groups and 12 placements for the Busks. Ch. Beau Monde The Huckster came upon the scene for Nancy

Bottom:
*Ch. Tres
Beau Decor*
was a
leading Non-
Sporting Dog
of the early
1980s
Owner,
George
Iverson.

Ch. Chaminade Tempo, by Petit Galant de St. George ex Ch. Reeneoy's Ami du Kilkanny, was a multiple Group winner of the mid- 1970s. Owned by Lois Morrow, Chamour Bichons, California.

Shapland with eight Groups and 28 placements. Iceman, now owned by Mrs. Cheever Porter, had a Best in Show, four Groups, and 38 placements. And C and D's Blue Moon of Crockerly had 25 Group placements for D. Siebert.

A new decade started with the 80's, and found Ch. Crockerly Beau Monde Eclipse number seven Non-Sporting Dog with a Best in Show, ten Groups, and 42 placements for Nancy Shapland. Ch. Teakas Erbin Einer was number ten Non-Sporting Dog with two Bests in Show and 40 Group placements, owned by J. Boston and L. Payne. Ch. Cameo Temptation Chaminade gained a Best in Show, two Groups, and 18 placements for J. and C. Denney and Mrs. Wm. Morrow. Ch. Norvic's Razzle Dazzle took a Best in Show, four Groups and 17 placements for Mrs. R. O'Keefe. Ch. Jalwin Just A Jiffy a Best in Show, seven Groups and 21 placements for P. and M. Schultz. Ch. Tres Beau Decor, eight Groups and 21 placements for G. Iverson. Iceman three Groups and 23 placements for Mrs. Porter. Ch. Rank's Raggedy Andy, three Groups and 16 placements for N. Makowiec and L. Brandman. Ch. Gay

The great and magnificent *Ch. Novic's Razzle Dazzle* was a multiple Group and Best in Show dog for Mr. Robert Koeppel.

Meadows Gage D'Amour, one Group, 12 placements, owner D. Moggack. Ch. Lambo of Lock Isle, one Best in Show, one Group, seven placements, owner D. Ayres.

Ch. Teakas Erbin Einer, owned by Judy Boston Payne, was number one Non-Sporting Dog in 1981 with 11 Bests in Show, 50 Group Firsts and 18 Group placements. Champion Jalwin Just A Jiffy was number three Non-Sporting Dog with six Bests in Show, 24 Group Firsts and 37 Group placements, owners P. and M. Schultz. Ch. Norvic's Razzle Dazzle was number ten Non-Sporting Dog with multi-Bests in Show, 11 Group Firsts and 27 Group placements, owner Robert Koeppel. And Ch. Tres Beau Decor was number 13 Non-Sporting Dog with two Bests in Show, ten Group Firsts and 26 Group placements.

In 1982 Ch. Teakas Erbin Einer was again top Bichon and number one Non-Sporting Dog with 18 Bests in Show, over 40 Group Firsts and 28 Group

Ch. Craigdale's Olé Rhondi, by Ch. D'Shar's Rendezvous du Chamour ex Ch. Wicked Music of Craigdale, was the #1 Bichon of 1983 and winner of eight Bests in Show, 60 Group One placements, and four Specialty Bests in Show. Olé has produced 18 champions, which include two Best in Show winners. Bred by Dale Hunter in Canada and owned by Lois Morrow. Photo courtesy of *Kennel Review*.

Champion
Craigdale's Olé Rhondi

Sire:
Ch. D'Shar Rendezvous Du Chamour

- Cameo Chaminade Chant
  - Ch. Chaminade Tempo
  - Ch. Jaclene's Chanadelle
- Ch. Braymar's Caprice Du Chaminade
  - Ch. Chaminade Tempo
  - Braymars Bali Hai

Dam:
Can. & Am. Ch. Wicked Music by Craigdale

- Ch. Vogel Flights Music Man
  - Ch. Chaminade Mr. Beau Monde
  - Ch. Vogel Flights Diandee Amy Pouf
- Beaumonde Works D'arte Renoir
  - Reenroy Sir Bernard
  - Works D'Arte Renoir

placements, Judy Boston Payne the owner. Ch. Hillwood Brass Band was in second place and also number nine Non-Sporting Dog with two Bests in Show and numerous Groups and placements, owner Ellen MacNeille.

The year 1983 ended with Ch. Craigdale's Olé Rhondi as Top Bichon and number three Non-Sporting dog and Ch. Paw Mark's Talk of the Town in second place with ten Group Firsts and 26 Group placements.

Then 1984 saw them reverse places with Talk of

Ch. Unicorn's Nickoles Nickelbee, #1 Bichon Frise in the United States in 1987 with seven Bests in Show, with his handler, Clifford Steel.

the Town in first place with nine Bests in Show, 35 Group Firsts and 52 Group placements and also second Top Non-Sporting Dog. While Olé was second with 22 Group Firsts and 40 Group placements. He also was number seven Non-Sporting Dog. Olé was owned by Lois Morrow and Barbara Stubbs and Talk of the Town by Pauline Schultz. In third place was Ch. Camelot Brassy Nickel, who had two Bests in Show, 15 Group Firsts and 29 Group placements. He was also number 15 Non-Sporting dog that year, owned by P. Goldman.

Ch. Devon Puff and Stuff was number one Bichon in 1985 as well as number one Non-Sporting dog with 20 Bests in Show, 51 Group Firsts and 34 Group placements. Ch. Tres Jolie Mr. Vagabond with one Best in Show, 14 Group Firsts and 35 Group placements came in as the number ten Non-Sporting dog in 1985 and was owned by L. Aronberg.

The year of 1986 saw Puff again as number one Bichon and number one Non-Sporting dog with 33 Bests in Show, 95 Group Firsts and 23 Group placements. Vagabond was second Bichon and eighth Non-Sporting dog with one Best in Show and 33 Group placements. In third place

RATOGA KENNEL CLUB

was Ch. Unicorn's Nicholas Nickelbee, who topped the list in 1987, breeder-owned by JoAnn Failla.

Ch. Devon Puff and Stuff
NS724478—America's top winning Bichon Frise of all time!

Born April 28, 1982, Female

Important wins:

Two Consecutive National Specialties

Two Consecutive Group One placements-Westminster Kennel Club, 1985 & 1986

Winner of Quaker Oats Award, 1986

Winner of Kennel Review Tournament of Champions, 1986

Winner of Purina Invitational, 1986

Winner of 60 All-Breed Bests in Show, 167 Group One placements; 58 Group Two placements; 24 Group Three placements; and 8 Group Four placements.

Winner of 267 career Bests of Breed, with 204 *consecutive* breed wins.

Best in Show Wins include: Kennel Club of Beverly Hills, International Kennel Club, Golden Gate Kennel Club, Astro Hall Shows, and many more.

Puff produced one litter, which produced three Champion bitches. Puff's outgoing temperament and enthusiasm are most noticeable in her daughters, but even more so in her

grandchildren. Her contributions will be evident for years to come through her outstanding grandsons, who are already siring champions and have several pointed get.

During her show career, Puff always seemed to recognize when that truly "something extra" was called for, and never failed to rise to the occasion. She possesses heart, enthusiasm, ring presence, and a zest for life that is seldom found in this, or indeed any, breed. As of this writing, she still retained all

Ch. Devon Puff and Stuff owned by Nancy Shapland a moment in the show ring. Miss Puff's total record consists of 60 all-breed Bests in Show; 167 Group One placements; and 267 Bests of Breed.

Ch. Devon Puff and Stuff, top winning Bichon in the History of the breed, is taking one of her 60 all-breed Bests in Show on this occasion in Arkansas. Her owner, Nancy Shapland of Champaign, Illinois, tells us that Miss Puff produced just one litter consisting of three champion bitches.

Ch. Devon Puff and Stuff

Registration No. NJ 724478

Sire:
Ch. Tomaura's
Moonlight Sonata

- Ch. Loftiss Reenie
  - Reenroy's Torro
  - Reenroy's Tanya
- Ch. Tomauca's Touch of Elegance
  - Ch. Tomaura's Frosty Snowman
  - Ch. Mainbrace Betsy of Tomaura

Dam:
Ch. C. and D.'s
Devon Hell's
Lil' Angel

- Ch. Chaminape Mr. Beau Monde
  - Ch. Cali-Col Robspierre
  - Ch. Reenroy's Ami Du Kilkanny
- Ch. C. and D.'s Countess Becky
  - Peppe De Barnette
  - Quentia of Goldysdale

Ch. Devon Puff and Stuff epitomizes so perfectly the merry, fun-loving, happy little dogs that Bichons have been since the beginning of time. Her owner, Nancy Shapland, says of her that Puff "possesses heart, enthusiasm, ring presence, and a zest for life that is seldom found in any breed."

of these wonderful attributes, even after the age of ten years old.

OFFICIAL STANDARD FOR THE BICHON FRISE

To purchase a Bichon Frise, no less to breed a Bichon Frise, you must know precisely what a good Bichon Frise looks like. Every registering organization, such as the American Kennel Club or the Kennel Club of England, adopts an official standard for the breed, a description of what the ideal representative of the breed should look like.

Standards, like purebred dogs for the most part, are manmade and man-remade, which is to say they change over time. These "word pictures" are subject not only to change but also to interpretation. In a perfect world, every breeder is striving for the flawless dog, which is identical in every way to the next breeder's flawless dog, which is identical in every way to the next breeder's flawless dog. In reality, however, the flawless dog doesn't exist, never has the never will. Nonetheless, breeders strive to create that "perfect speciman" and smart owners strive to find that "perfect puppy."

Read the following breed standard carefully and repeatedly. Envision every

This is the well-known *Ch. Sea Star Wicked Destiny*, son of Ch. Diament's Le Magnifique ex Ch. Balderne Fleur Lalique. Bred by Mrs. Jill Cohen in California, Destiny is co-owned by Ellen MacNeille and Pam Goldman for whom Clifford Steel is the handler.

part of the dog and ask an experienced breeder or exhibitor about anything you don't understand completely.

When buying a puppy, you should know what to look for and NOT to look for. Pay close attention to disqualifications and faults. When considering gait, remember that your puppy is but a "toddler"; instead observe the movement of the parents or other relatives. Structure as well as movement are passed along from parent to offspring.

GENERAL APPEARANCE—
The Bichon Frise is a small, sturdy, white powder puff of a dog whose merry temperament is evidenced by his plumed tail carried jauntily over the back and his dark-eyed inquisitive expression. This is a breed that has no gross or incapacitating exaggerations and therefore there is no inherent reason for lack of balance or unsound movement. Any deviation from the ideal described in the standard should be penalized to the extent of the deviation. Structural faults common to all breeds are as undesirable in the Bichon Frise as in any toher breed, even though such faults may not be specifically mentioned in the standard.

Size, Proportion, Substance
    Size— Dogs and bitches $9^1/_2$ to $11^1/_2$ inches are to be given primary preference.

Only where the comparative superiority of a specimen outside this range clearly justifies it should greater latitude be taken. In no case, however, should this latitude ever extend over 12 inches or under 9 inches. The minimum limits do not apply to puppies.
    Proportion— The body from the forward-most point of the chest to the point of rump is $^1/_4$ longer than the height at the withers. The body from the withers to lowest point of chest represents $^1/_2$ the distance from withers to ground.
    Substance— Compact and of medium bone throughout, neither coarse nor fine.

Best of Breed at York Kennel Club in 1989 was *Ch. Windstars Goddess of Love.* Sired by Ch. Efaldee's Always A Challenge ex Ch. Windstars Alexis D'Carrington, this consistent Breed and Group winner belongs to Mr. Robert A. Koeppel and her handler is Wendy Kellerman.

Head

Expression— Soft, dark-eyed, inquisitive, alert. *Eyes* are round, black or dark brown and are set in the skull to directly forward. An overly large or bulging eye is a fault as is an almond shaped, obliquely set eye. Halos, the black or very dark brown skin surrounding the eyes, are necessary as they accentuate the eye and enhance expression. The eye rims themselves must be black. Broken pigment, or total absence of pigment on the eye rims produce a bland and staring expression, which is a definite fault. Eyes of any color other than black or dark brown are a very serious fault and must be severely penalized. *Ears* are drop and are covered with long flowing hair. When extended toward the nose, the leathers reach approximately halfway the length of the muzzle. They are set on slightly higher than eye level and rather forward on the skull, so that when the dog is alert they serve to frame the face. The *skull* is slightly rounded, allowing for a round and forward looking eye. The *stop* is slightly accentuated. *Muzzle*— A properly balanced head is three parts muzzle to five parts skull, measured from the nose to the stop and from the stop to the occiput. A line drawn between the outside corners of the eyes and to the nose will create a near equilateral triangle. There is a slight degree of chiseling under the eyes, but not so much as to result in a weak or snipy foreface. The lower jaw is strong. The *nose* is prominent and always black. *Lips* are black, fine, never drooping. *Bite* is scissors. A bite which is undershot or overshot

should be severely penalized. A crooked or out of line tooth is permissible, however, missing teeth are to be severely faulted.

Neck, Topline and Body

The arched **neck** is long and carried proudly behind an erect head. It blends smoothly into the shoulders. The length of neck from occiput to withers is approximately $\frac{1}{3}$ the distance from forechest to buttocks. The **topline** is level except for a slight, muscular arch over the loin. **Body**— The chest is well developed and wide enough to allow free and unrestricted movement of the front legs. The lowest point of the chest extends at least to the elbow. The rib cage is moderately sprung and extends back to a short and muscular loin. The forechest is well pronounced and protrudes slightly forward of the point of shoulder. The underline has a moderate tuck-up. **Tail** is well plumed, set on level with the topline and curved gracefully over the back so that the hair of the tail rests on the back. When the tail is extended toward the head it reaches at least halfway to the withers. A low tail set, a tail carried perependicularly to the back, or a tail which droops behind is to be severely penalized. A corkscrew tail is a very serious fault.

Forequarters

Shoulders— The shoulder blade, upper arm

Ch. Aldo's What About Bob at age one year becomes a new champion at the Sarnia Kennel Club event. Bred and owned by Doug Buckingham and Alec White, and handled by Doug, he is a Damien 1st son nicely endowed with the thick plush coat that is an asset to this line.

Ch. Glen Elfred Fountainbleu is handled here by Toby Fresch, who co-owns this lovely bitch with Eleanor Grassick, to the exciting victory of Winners Bitch at Westminster in 1988. Sired by Ch. Bunnyrun Going Nova, ROM ex Ch. Glen Elfred Merry Magnaux, "Tia" was the Bichon Frise Club of America Dam of the Year for 1991. She was bred by Eleanor Grassick and Laurie Klieger.

and forearm are approximately equal in length. The shoulders are laid back to somewhat near a forty-five degree angle. The upper arm extends well back so the elbow is placed directly below the withers when viewed from the side. *Legs* are of medium bone; straight, with no bow or curve in the forearm or wrist. The elbows are held close to the body. The *pasterns* slope slightly from the vertical. The dewclaws may be removed. The *feet* are tight and round, resembling those of a cat and point directly forward, turning neither in nor out. *Pads* are black. *Nails* are kept short.

Hindquarters

The hindquarters are of medium bone, well angulated with muscular thighs and spaced moderately wide. The upper and lower thigh are nearly equal in length meeting at a well bent stifle joint. The leg from hock joint to foot pad is perpendicular to the ground. Dewclaws may be removed. Paws are tight and round with black pads.

Coat

The texture of the coat is of utmost importance. The undercoat is soft and dense, the outercoat of a coarser and curlier texture. The combination of the two gives a soft but substantial feel to the touch which is similar to plush or velvet and when patted springs back. When bathed and brushed, it stands off the body, creating an overall powder puff appearance. A wiry coat is not desirable. A limp, silky coat, a coat that lies down, or a lack of undercoat are very serious faults. *Trimming*— The coat is trimmed to reveal the natural outline of the body. It is rounded off from any direction and never cut so short as to create an overly trimmed or squared off appearance. The furnishings of the head, beard, mustache, ears and tail are left longer. The longer head hair is trimmed to create an overall rounded impression. The topline is trimmed to appear level. The coat is long enough to maintain the powder puff look which is characteristic of the breed.

Color

Color is white, may have shadings of buff, cream, or apricot around the ears or on the body. Any color in excess of 10% of the entire coat of a mature specimen is a fault and should be penalized, but color of the accepted shadings should not be faulted in puppies.

Gait

Movement at a trot is free, precise, and effortless. In profile the forelegs and hind legs extend equally with an easy reach and drive that maintain a steady topline. When moving, the head and neck remain somewhat erect and as speed increases there is a very slight convergence of legs toward the center line. Moving away, the hindquarters travel with moderate width between them and the foot pads can be seen. Coming and going, his movement is precise and true.

Temperament

Gentle mannered, sensitive, playful and affectionate. A cheerful attitude is the hallmark of the breed and one should settle for nothing less.

Approved October 11, 1988

Ch. Doriann's Pegasus won Group One placement at the Long Island Kennel Club in 1991. Sired by Ch. Whitegolds Razzberry Jubilee ex Ch. Doriann's Starburst, Pegasus was bred by Doriann Bichons and belongs to Mr. Robert A. Koeppel. Handled by Wendy Kellerman. Pegasus was #5 Bichon for 1990 and 1991.

Ch. Le Beau Chien Glenelfred TNT owned by Eleanor Grassick.

Ch. Titan de Wanabry owned by Mrs. Celeste Fleishman.

Ch. Glen Elfred's Billy Boy bred by Laurie Klieger and Eleanor Grassick.

Ch. Pepin de Staramour owned by Mrs. Celeste Fleishman.

Ch. Ballade du Babette owned by Eleanor Grassick.

Ch. Hanna's Trustin Tovar owned by Mrs. Celeste Fleishman.

Top: *Ch. Hillwood's Beausnost of Camelot* winning Best of Breed at Long Island Kennel Club in 1992. Handled by Cliff Steel for owner Mrs. Pam Goldman. This handsome little dog was Winners Dog at the Bichon Frise Club of America National Specialty in 1991 and has many outstanding successes to his credit. Bottom: *Ch. Pillow Talk's Carte Blanche* by Ch. Montravia Jazz-M-Tazz, ROMX ex Ch. Pillow Talk's Kissin' Fool. This dog finished his championship by going Winners Dog at Westchester in 1992 with his fourth major. Owner-handled to all points by Lori Kornfeld, co-owned by Tracy Kornfeld.

Top: *Ch. Fran-Dor's Esprit Enjoue* winning Best of Breed at Penn Treaty Kennel Club in 1984. Sired by Ch. Miri-Cal's Motet ex Ch. Fran- Dor's Athena. A dog of type and quality, he, like his sire, did much splendid winning for his owners Ed and Anne Jones, Charles, Virginia. Bottom: *Ch. Dreams Come True Jennifer* owned by Mimi Winkler.

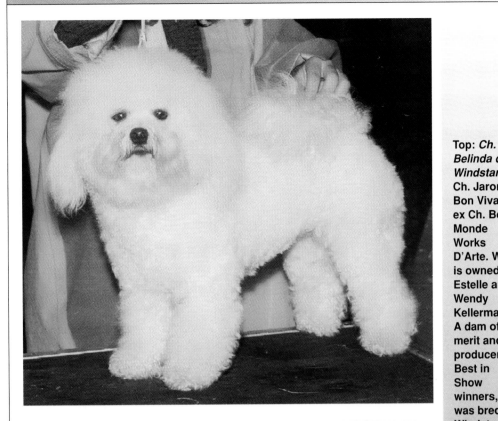

Top: *Ch. Belinda de Windstar* by Ch. Jaronda Bon Vivant ex Ch. Beau Monde Works D'Arte. Witty is owned by Estelle and Wendy Kellerman. A dam of merit and a producer of Best in Show winners, she was bred by Windstar Bichons. Belinda was enroute to her championship in this 1977 photo. Bottom: *Ch. Glen Elfred's Firefly* is owned by Robert Koepell.

Bichons in Great Britain

As could easily have been anticipated, it took but a short time for dog lovers of the United Kingdom to see and evaluate the charm and beauty of the Bichon Frise and come to the decision that they, too, wished to participate in the owning and breeding of these delightful little dogs.

Thus it was that during the early 1970s the British were making plans for acquisition of excellent foundation stock from both the United States and continental breeders in France and Belgium. The British gave thoughtful study to the manner in which they might be used most successfully. For after all, the British traditionally bred great dogs and they were anxious to have their Bichons live up to these ideals.

The first British purchase toward establishment of the Bichon Frise in England was from the United States in 1973, headed for the Carlise Kennels belonging to Mr. and Mrs. J. Sorstein. Two of them were Rava's Real Valor of Reenroy, sired by Stardom's Odim Rex, Jr., and Jenny Vive de Carlise, a daughter of the Odin Rex son, Beauchaun High Cotton ex Snobee de Beauchaun.

A year later, during 1974, the first British-born litter of Bichons arrived from Real Valor and Jenny Viva. Among them was the dog who became Ch. Carlise Cicero of Tresilva. This dog later helped get the breed established in Australia after doing so in Great Britain.

Cicero's sister, Carlise Circe of Tresilva, accompanied him to the Tresilva Kennels. At this same time Mrs. Jackie Ransom also brought in the first two imports from Belgium to England, these being Zethus de Chaponay of Tresilva and Zena de Chapony of Tresilva.

Zena, in due course, was bred to Cicero with exciting results. One of these lovely litters included the famous and influential Int. Ch. Tresilva Don Azur and his sister Tresilva Donna Azur.

Having put his stamp on the British Bichons, Cicero was sold to Australia, where his influential quality and bloodlines again proved an asset.

Mrs. Ransom is widely admired and respected as a member of the British dog fancy, where she remains active as a writer (among her works an outstanding book on Bichons), an

Eng. Am. Ch. Sibon Sloane Ranger at Pamplona was bred by Mrs. Marion Binder, and purchased by Michael Coad who later sold him to Mrs. Jill Cohen at Sea Star Kennels in Malibu, California. Upon arrival at his new home in the States, Sloan Ranger completed his American Championship title within 36 hours!

Eng. and Ir. Ch. Tiopepi Mad Louie won the Toy Group at Crufts. Only one of the many outstanding victories on the record of this magnificent dog. Geoff Corish handling for owner Michael Coad.

English Irish Champion
Tiopepi Mad Louie At Pamplona

Sire: Ch. Montravia Persan Make Mine Mink

- Int. Ch. If De La Buthiere of Antarctica
  - Fr. Ch. U-Sam De Villa Sainval
  - Fr. Ch. Urfee De La Buthiere
- Leander Pleasures Persan
  - Aust. Ch. Huntglen Leander Arden
  - Beau Monde The Ripple Of Leander

Dam: Leijazulip Sabina of Colhamdorn

- Eng. Aust. Ch. Jazz De La Buthiere of Leijazulip
  - Int. Ch. If De La Buthiere Of Antarctica
  - Ch. Vanda De La Buthiere
- Carlises Calypso Orion
  - Rava's Regal Valor of Reenroy
  - Jenny Vive De Carlise

Eng. Ch. Kynismar Blackeyed Boogaloo, an important British winner of ten Challenge Certificates, nine Bests of Breed, and many Group One placements. Boogaloo is by Shamaney Stepping Out at Kynismar ex Eng. Ch. Kynismar Blackeyed Susie. Owner, Mrs. Aikins, Effingham, Surrey.

owner of Bichons, and a widely in-demand multiple breed dog show judge who officiates frequently at home and abroad.

The breeding of that first English-born litter was later repeated, again providing foundation stock for more new fanciers, in this case Derek Chiverton and Vera Goold. They purchased Carlise Calypso Orion, who later became grandsire of the phenomenally successful Ch. Tiopepi Mad Louie at Pamplona, a world leader in the breed.

Another from this Carlise litter went to a very well-known Pekingese breeder, Betty Mirylees of the Beaupres Kennels. Ms.

Mirylees eventually sold him to the Glenfolly Kennels owned by Chris Cooley, in New Zealand, thus becoming the first Bichon in that country.

It was in 1975 that the above mentioned Mrs. Goold brought to England, from France, two stunning Bichons destined to make history on a worldwide scale from the kennels of the great French breeder of Bichons, Mme. Desfarge. These were the superb dog Jazz de la Buthiere of Leijazulip and the gorgeous bitch Leilah de la Buthiere. These two left admirable accomplishments behind them in England when they were sold to Australia. They enjoyed equally spectacular

Ir. Ch. Pamplona Gay Crusader was "Dog of the Year" in Ireland in 1988 and was later exported to Wendy Streatfield of Leander fame in South Africa where he became Top Toy in 1989. Owned in Great Britain by Michael Coad.

success as they continued to produce impressive quality while gaining notable show records there.

A son of Jazz and Leilah, Leijazulip Guillaume, gained wide acclaim and International Championships after being sold to and campaigned by a fancier in Sweden. His credits as a stud dog there as well as in England also add up impressively.

A whole series of famous and influential Bichons are owned by Myra and Robert Aikens of Effingham in Surrey. This kennel is

another whose contributions to Bichons have been and continue to be significant, gaining for Mrs. Aikens an enviable reputation for expertise and knowledge in this breed.

Mrs. Aikens' first homebred champion was the outstanding and famed

Ch. Kynismar Blackeyed Susie. Then came the prepotent and gorgeous son of Susie, Ch. Kynismar Blackeyed Boogaloo, who became the sire of four champion sons. Boogaloo is among the leading Bichon show dogs in England, having ten Challenge Certificates, nine Bests of Breed, and a Variety Group first to his credit at time of writing. Also he was the Top Winning Stud Dog among all Toy breeds for 1989.

Leander kennels, owned by John and Wendy Streatfield, have established themselves well in the Bichon world as breeders and as importers of famous and high quality Bichons, many of whom go on to help establish kennels in other parts of the world. Originally Poodle people, it took them little time once they had met their first Bichon to gain high admiration for that breed. As of now their contribution has been inestimable.

The Streatfield's first Bichon came to them in 1974, a magnificent bitch who did much for the breed. She was followed by numerous others of historical importance, including the famed Ch. Vogelflight's Choir Boy.

The Streatfields acquired principally from the

The widely acclaimed *Eng. Ch. Sibon Fatal Attraction at Pamplona* is the current Bichon Frise record holder in England with 31 Challenge Certificates, and is the first Bichon bitch ever to go Best in Show at a General Championship Dog Show in the UK. Additionally she has won 22 Group One placements, and was "Dog of the Year" in 1990 thus becoming the first Bichon Frise ever to win this award. Owner, Michael Coad, Longton, Lancs.

western United States, especially Chaminade, Beau Monde, C and D, and Vogelflight. But they also imported from the de la Buthiere and Closmyons kennels in France, thus their own Leander breeding program is a combination of the finest from both worlds.

We understand that Mrs. Streatfield, probably due to being a Poodle lady, quickly noticed the lack of grooming style in the early British Bichons. It was she who created a style of grooming for them that resulted in far more elegantly turned-out Bichons than the little curly ragamuffin look of the continent. The new style was well received both in Great Britain and in Australia, where it was brought by Leander dogs and promptly adopted.

The arrival of Michael Coad and Geoffrey Cornish in Great Britain's Bichon world was indeed the start of something really big for the little white dogs there. Not that Michael and Geoffrey were any strangers to the dog show world as they had successfully been "in" dogs for about ten years at their time of "Bichon discovery." But they had not met Bichons earlier.

Then one day Michael made the discovery while visiting a Poodle friend, Clair Coxhall, owner of the "Tiopepis" who was then breeding Bichons, too. She invited him to look at her current Bichon litter. The puppies were ten weeks old, but even that early one in particular caught Michael's eye. By the time he left there that day, the puppy was his who grew up to become the wonderful Mad Louie!

As he matured, the qualities that had first attracted Michael became steadily pronounced. Ultimately he was ready to take on the dog show world, in which he became Ch. Tiopepi Mad Louie at Pamplona, the first Bichon to achieve Best in Show at a British Championship Dog Show.

Mad Louie has produced champions galore, as well as leading winners in all parts of the Bichon world. In addition to England, his progeny has seen success in Australia, Denmark, Holland, Ireland, Norway, South Africa and Sweden.

Among Louie's gorgeous show kids is Pamplona's Gay Crusader, who gained his championship in Ireland. He was on the way to go for his English title when Mrs. Streatfield saw him and immediately wanted him to take with her to South Africa. Geoffrey and Michael of course agreed, and Crusader became a Top-Ten Toy there.

Then another Louie offspring, Eng. and Am. Ch. Sibon Sloan Ranger, at age eight months, impressed visiting USA handler Lesley Boyes so deeply that she wanted to take him home with her to her client, Mrs. Jill Cohen in California. Finally it all worked out and Sloan Ranger came to Mrs. Cohen on the completion of his British Championship.

We feel certain that one of Britain's major success stories of the dog show world must be that of the remarkable Bichon female, Ch. Sibon's Fatal Attraction. An exquisite example of Bichon correctness and beauty, Fatal gained admirers wherever she appeared. She is the culmination of what one seeks in a Bichon, one and all evidently agreed, as never a dissenting word has reached my ears even with all the Bichon folks I've talked with in the preparation of this book.

Michael and Geoff, of course, have presented her flawlessly on her ring appearances, despite the extra care and attention required when one's show dog is actually a bitch. But Fatal's assets are so outstanding and her excellence so incomparable that even though they had misgivings when they started out with her, they were quickly overcome.

Fatal belongs to Mrs. Bender, who must be a proud and happy lady over the success she has had with this little Bichon on the highly competitive British Dog Show scene. Fatal won her first Challenge Certificate at the famous Windsor Dog Show, the other two for her championship following in rapid succession.

When the smoke of battle had cleared from the area of Bichons in the English show rings, Fatal Attraction had amassed a total of 33 Challenge Certificates and 22 Toy Groups. She was named Dog of the Year in Great Britain for 1990.

In retrospect, the Bichon Frise Club of Great Britain was organized during 1976. It held its first specialty show in 1982. The Northern and Midland Bichon Frise Club was the next approved, during March 1982. And the third organized, the Bichon Frise Breeders Association, came after that.

BRITISH STANDARD

General Appearance
Well balanced dog of smart appearance, closely

Above: *Ch. Sibon Fatal Attraction* has gone Best in Show twice, including a Best in Show at the National Specialty in Great Britain. Owner, Michael Coad. Left: Michael Coad handling and winning with *Ch. Sibon Fatal Attraction*, leading winner among the Bichons of the UK.

coated with handsome plume carried over the back. Natural white coat curling loosely. Head carriage proud and high.

Characteristics
Gay, happy, lively little dog.

Temperament
Friendly and outgoing.

Head and Skull
Ratio of muzzle length to skull length 3:5. On a head of the correct width and length, lines drawn between the outer corners of the eyes and nose will create a near equilateral triangle. Whole head in balance with body. Muzzle not thick, heavy nor snipey. Cheeks flat, not very strongly muscled. Stop moderate but definite, hollow between eyebrows just visible. Skull slightly rounded, not coarse, with hair accentuating rounded appearance. Nose large, round, black, soft and shiny.

Eng. Ch. Kynismar Cherished Heaven was the eighth Bichon to complete title for Mrs. M. Aikins, Effingham, Surrey, England. Sired by Ch. Kynismar Billy The Kid ex Eng. Ch. Kynismar Heaven Sent, this very handsome Bichon belongs to and was bred by Mrs. M. Aikins, Effingham, Surrey.

Eyes
Dark, round with black eye rims, surrounded by dark haloes, consisting of well pigmented skin. Forward-looking, fairly large but not almond-shaped, neither obliquely set nor protruding. Showing no white when looking forward. Alert, full of expression.

Ears
Hanging close to head, well covered with flowing hair longer than leathers, set on slightly higher than eye level and rather forward on skull. Carried forward when dog alert, forward edge touching skull. Leather reaching approximately half-way along muzzle.

Mouth
Jaws strong, with a perfect regular and complete scissor bite, i.e. upper teeth closely overlapping lower teeth and set square to the jaws. Full dentition desirable. Lips fine, fairly tight and completely black.

Neck
Arched neck fairly long, about one-third the length of the body. Carried high and proudly. Round and slim near head, gradually broadening to fit smoothly into shoulders.

Eng. Ir. Ch. Tiopepi Mad Louis at Pamplona, photographed with Michael Coad.

Forequarters

Shoulders oblique, not prominent, equal in length to upper arm. Upper fits close to body. Legs straight, perpendicular, when seen from front; not too finely boned. Pasterns short and straight viewed from front, very slightly sloping viewed from side.

Body

Forechest well developed, deep brisket. Ribs well sprung, floating ribs not terminating abruptly. Loin broad, well muscled, slightly arched and well tucked up. Pelvis broad, croup slightly rounded. Length from withers to tailset should equal height from withers to ground.

Hindquarters

Thighs broad and well rounded. Stifles well bent; hocks well angulated and metatarsals perpendicular.

Feet

Tight, rounded and well knuckled up. Pads black. Nails preferably black.

Tail

Normally carried raised and curved gracefully over the back but not tightly curled. Never docked. Carried in line with backbone, only hair touching back; tail itself not in contact. Set on level with topline, neither too high nor too low. Corkscrew tail undesirable.

Gait/Movement

Balanced and effortless with an easy reach and drive maintaining a

Eng. Am. Ch. Sibon Sloan Ranger owned by Mrs. Jill Cohen of Malibu, California. Photo courtesy of his former owner Michael Coad.

steady and level topline. Legs moving straight along line of travel, with hind pads showing.

Coat
Fine, silky with soft corkscrew curls. Neither flat nor corded, and measuring 7-10 cm (3-4 ins) in length. The dog may be presented untrimmed or have muzzle and feet slightly tidied up.

Colour
White, but cream or apricot markings acceptable up to 18 months. Under white coat, dark pigment desirable. Black, blue or beige markings often found on skin.

Size
Ideal height: 23-28 cms (9-11 ins) at withers.

Faults
Any departure from the foregoing points should be considered a fault and the seriousness with which the fault should be regarded should be in exact proportion to its degree.

Note
Male animals should have two apparently normal testicles fully descended into the scrotum.

Top: Flower Boy bred by Mrs. Pauline Block in Hampshire England exported this lovely young male to Canada.

Delightful puppies, age 6 weeks, from Mrs. M. Aikins famed kennel at Effingham, Surrey, England. These two were sired by Eng. Ch. Kynismar Heaven Forbid ex Love Letters From Kynismar.

Top: *Eng. Ch. Kynismar Blackeyed Mr. Magoo* was the winner of Best Bichon Dog at Crufts in 1990. By Shamaney Steppin Out at Kynismar ex Eng. Ch. Kynismar Blackeyed Susie, he was bred by Mrs. Aikins, Effingham, Surrey. Bottom: Judge Andrew Brace with the Crufts Challenge-Certificate-winning bitch, *Ir. Ch. Eithlynn Vanessa* owned by Mrs. L.M. Clarke, who went on to Best of Breed. On the right is the dog Challenge Certificate victor, *Ch. Hylacen's Northern Topic*, belonging to Mr. and Mrs. L.V. Dickinson and B. Dickinson.

At Crufts, 1994, judge Andrew Brace goes over his eventual Best of Breed, *Ir. Ch. Eithlynn Vanessa*. Owner/handler, Mrs. L.M. Clarke.

A day at the famous Crufts Dog Show, 1989. *Ch. Kynismar Heaven Sent* was the winner of Best Bitch and Best of Breed, while her brother, *Ch. Kynismar Boogie's Boy*, won Best Dog, making it a "double." Owned by Mrs. M. Aikins, Effingham, Surrey.

Top: *Twinley Secret Combination* looks ready for anything! One of the delightful Bichons owned in England by Mrs. Pauline Block, Whitchurch, Hamps. Bottom: A fabulous litter of eight baby Bichons from England courtesy of the noted breeder, multi- breed judge and author of dog books, Mrs. Jackie Ransom who resides at Wembley Park, Middlesex. These babies are by Tresilva Virgil ex Tresilva Lovable at Suanalu, and are a splendid example of the superior quality to be found at Mrs. Ransom's long-established Tresilva Kennels.

Eng. Ch. Kynismar Heaven Sent pictured winning Best of Breed at Crufts, England's greatest dog show, in 1989. This outstanding homebred English champion has 22 Challenge Certificates plus three Group placements among other prestigious successes. Bred by Mrs. M. Aikins, Effingham, Surrey.

Bichons in Canada

History tells us that the first Bichons Frises to reach Canada did so sometime shortly before 1967 (when the first litter on Canadian soil was born) to a Mr. McLean, who bred Poodles under the "Wildboy" identification at his home near Calgary. The Bichons came to Mr. McLean from Woodlinville, Washington. They were sold to him by Mrs. Goldy Olsen from her imported de La Roche Posay bloodlines. This dog and this bitch represented excellent French bloodlines. The aforementioned first Canadian litter gave to Mr. McLean one bitch and four males.

Other activity within the breed during that same period of Canadian Bichon history included a pair of them brought to Nova Scotia by Mrs. Muriel Ven Veniot of Kingston. This same lady also imported, at age nine weeks, the male Ulric de Villa Sainval from the famous Belgian authorities Mr. and Mrs. Albert Baras of Tilft, Belgium.

Bichons involved in other Canadian purchases during the 1960s-70s period included Quinsel of Goldsy'dale and Quette of Goldsy'dale. So far as we are able to ascertain, there have been no significant activities recorded for those early breeders since the beginning.

The best friend ever for the Bichon Frise in Canada has been Mrs. Kay

Calderbank, herself a Bichon breeder of tremendous dedication and energy. Her own Myworth Kennel in British Columbia was founded on her first three purchases from Goldy Olsen's de La Roche Posay line and plus de Gascoigne, de Wanabry, Steren Vor and Frimousette. Then in 1972 she imported Can. and Am.

Ch. Ee's R Regal Prince of Henruf (Petit Galant de St. George ex Cali-Col's Ritzy Ruffles), who was to have tremendous impact on the breed in Canada.

Mrs. Calderbank was the breeder of Can. and Am. Ch. Myworth's Enchantment, the breed's Top Winner and Top Producing sire. Widely praised by scores of his

This photo was made at the first Booster Show following formation of the Bichon Frise Club of Canada. Kay Calderbank, the lady who has so widely contributed to and assisted progress of this breed in Canada, is pictured here, the fourth person kneeling from the left. Photo courtesy of Dale Hunter, North Vancouver, British Columbia.

Am. Can. Ch. Wicked Music by Craigdale is the dam of Craigdale Olé Rhondi. This lovely headstudy photographed by Missy Yuhl is courtesy of Dale Hunter.

admirers, he was the first Bichon to win a Canadian Best in Show. Between 1976 and 1978, Enchantment won 12 Bests in Show, 39 Groups, 76 placements, and Best of Breed on 128 occasions. He was by Ch. My Windy K ex Ch. Lejerdell Tar-Esa.

During that time when Bichons in America had been keeping their own registry, handled by the Bichon Frise Club of America, Canadian fanciers had joined the BFCA in order to be able to list their Canadian-bred litters and imports in that registry. All went smoothly until the American Kennel Club, in preparation for the United States Bichons receiving official recognition from the AKC as a breed, took over their registry from the American Specialty Club, which closed that source of registration to the Canadians. Then they needed to get busy on forming their own Canadian Specialty Club, thus creating a registry of their own in preparation for eventual CKC approval. Mrs. Calderbank worked long and hard helping with this movement, both with impressing everyone with its importance and getting at the work that would bring it about. Much needed doing to assure the future of Canadian Bichons, as one realizes the fact that in 1971 only 19 Bichons existed in that entire country. But all went well, and our little friend the Bichon's position as a recognized breed was approved by the Canadian Kennel Club in March of 1975.

Surprisingly to many, the Bichon Frise Club of Canada did not come into existence until four years after the breed was applied and accepted by the Canadian Kennel Club. That made it 1979 when the Bichon Frise Club of Canada came into existence. Since then it has flourished and been joined by some extremely energetic hardworking regional clubs as well, these having been formed in various sections of the country. Officials of the national club itself included, as President, Carole Mineault of Sussex, N.B.; a very active and still involved past President, Norma Dirszowsky, Udora, Ontario, who also serves as editor of the club's splendid official publication, *Bichon Banter*, published quarterly and supplied free of charge to club members.

The first male Bichon to gain championship in Canada was Ch. Lejerdell's Tar-Get of Myworth, son of Ch. Tarzan de la Persaliere ex Sarriete de Wanabry. The first Bichon female to make championship was Ch. Lejerdell's Tar-Esa, also by Tarzan.

Numerous Canadian kennels have now contributed significantly to the Bichon in Canada today, and some magnificent ones are to be found there these breeders can well take pride. I am certain the readers will realize as they study the photos and captions of this book. For example there is Dale Hunter, owner of the Craigdales in British Columbia, whose foundation bitch was Beau Monde Works d'Arte Wicked, by Reenroy Sir Bernard ex Works d'Arte Renoir. From a breeding to Ch. Vogelflight's Music Man she was dam of Can. and

Ch. Trevor's Miss Mandy, winning the Best Brood Bitch, at the Bichon Frise Club of Canada Specialty in 1985, with her three offspring: *Ch. Trevor's Damien 1st*, who won the Specialty; *Amber*, as Reserve Winners Bitch; and *Tiffany*, as Best Puppy in Show. The owner is Joan Trevor.

Can. Ch. Hooligan's Dreammaker owned by Sandra Lyn Dawson, Hooligan Bichons, Okoroks, Alberta. Dreammaker is the foundation bitch at Hooligan Kennels. Among her noted offspring are Can. Ch. Hooligan's Master of the Game and from her second litter, Can. Ch. Hooligan's Winsome Southern Bell, Sunberry Boy, And Topy Boy.

Can. Ch. Hooligan Winsome Southern Bell winning Best Puppy in Show at Northern Alberta Canine Association in October 1991. Bred by Ethel and Sandra Lyn Dawson; owned by Sandra Lyn Dawson.

Ch. Hooligan's Winsome Toy Boy looking very much the successful winner as he "sets up" to accept his Best of Breed award in July 1992. Toy Boy belongs to Debbie McFarlane, Bragg Creek, Alberta.

Hooligan's Tarnished Angel, bred by Ethel and Sandra Lyn Dawson of Okotoks, Alberta, is owned by Sandra Lyn Dawson and is pictured winning Best Puppy in Breed in July 1990.

Am. Ch. Wicked Music by Craigdale, the dam of five champions. One of the latter was Can. and Am. Ch. Craigdale's Olé Rhondi (sired by D'Shar's Rendezvous du Chamour, who along with being a

Barbara Stubbs and Lois Morrow through his descendants).

Ch. Craigdale Great Classic, by Ch. Cali-Col's Beau Monde ex Beau Monde Works d'Arte Wicked, bred to Can. and

Garda Johnstone owns this handsome Canadian Group winner, *Am. Can. Ch. Craigdale And The Sundance Kid*. Photo courtesy of Dale Hunter, North Vancouver.

multi-Best in Show winner was Top Bichon in the U.S. for 1983 and figures prominently in the current breeding program of

Am. Ch. Tarawn's Cheyenne Sundance (Vande le Buthiere-ex Myworth Miss Muffett) produced Can. and Am.

Am. Ca. Ch. *Wendar Fly The Flag* owned by Anne Yokum of Sidney, British Columbia. "Pilot, " as he is known, started a highly successful career during 1991, in which he ammassed 43 Group One placements and six all-breed Bests in Show. When that year ended, Pilot had gained the honor of being the first Bichon in Canada to have acquired "the most points in a year," which he did by a very wide margin.

Am. Can. Ch. Wendar Fly The Flag

Registration No. 1033961

Sire:
Eng. Irish Ch.
  Tiopepi Mad Louie
  At Pamplona

- Ch. Montravia Make Mine Mink
  - Ch. If De La Buthiere of Antarctica
  - Leander Pleasures Persan
- Leij. Sabina Of Calhamdorn
  - Eng. Aust. Ch. JazzDe La Buthiere of Leijazulip
  - Carlises Calypso Orion

Dam:
White Sprite At
  Wendar

- Effaldees Precious Oliver at Garbosa
  - Ligray Percious Gift
  - Ligray The Aristocrat
- Bright Idea of Mondolyn
  - Effaldees Tramp Around Town
  - Zudiki Snow Bird

Top: *Can. Am. Ch. Trevor's Damien*, bred and owned by Joan Trevor. Bottom: *Can. Ch. Kenningway's Hairy Baby*, winning Best in Show owned by Florence E. Erwin, Mississauga, Ontario.

Ch. Craigdale and the Sundance Kid, magnificent Group winner belonging to Garda Johnstone.

Anne Yokum must take deep pride in her wonderful little dog, Am. and Can. Ch. Wyndar Fly the Flag, Canada's Top Bichon in 1992, who was also the winner of "more points than any other dog in Canada" in 1991, the first time this distinction had been gained in Canada by a Bichon, and by a very wide margin.

Kendra James of Regina, Saskatchewan, has a truly lovely and distinguished bitch among the others of her Bichons in Ch. Kenningway's Hairy Baby,

a promonent winner, too.

Joan Trevor is one of Canada's leading Bichon breeders with some enviable achievements. Her homebreds include Can. and Am. Ch. Trevor's Damien 1st, a multi-Best in Show winner and also Best in Specialty at two Canadian Nationals in 1985 and 1986. Joan has bred numerous other worthy champions as well, and you will note a number of them through our pages.

During a recent judging trip to Canada, it was my pleasure to judge a splendid Booster Show for Bichons at Limestone, every moment of which we enjoyed. There we became acquainted with Harriet Cadott of Glenburnie, Ontario, whose dogs are of

excellent type and which I greatly admired. This is a knowledgeable and dedicated lady, another who is doing well for her breed.

Merville Landry and his wife Marguerite are a delightful couple who have been most cordial and helpful in sending wonderful photos to be used here. Mr. Landry himself is writing a most comprehensive three-volume study of the Bichon that we all will enjoy. He is such a dedicated person that just talking with him about his beloved breed is exciting. The Landrys own FranBel Bichons at New Brunswick, and were owners of the renowned and many titled German, French, European, Luxembourg, International, World and Canadian Ch. Pablo de la Buthiere from that illustrious kennel in France. Pablo came to Canada with the Landrys at age five years and shared their home until his death at age 11. Merville Landry describes Pablo as "the dog of my life." He was noted for a thick, pure white coat, very good pigmentation, and 10 1/2 inches height at the withers. His photos are doubly interesting both due to his influence in Canada

Ger., Fr., Eur, Lux., Int., World and Can. Ch. Pablo de la Buthiere. Pablo was the son of Fr. and Int. Ch. U-Sam de Villa-Sainval ex Fr. and Int. Ch. Natacha de La Buthiere. Born in France on June 21, 1979, his breeder was Mrs. Carmen Desfarges. Owned by Mr. Merville and Mrs. Marguerite Landry.

Ch. Talewagons Klassy Keke. Owned and bred by Shirley M. Baxter, Talewagon Bichons, Willowdale, Ontario.

Can. Ch. John Ann Lindy Lu of Cadott. Owner, Harriet Cadott.

Am. Can. Ch. Valentine's Shelsea Lascell owned by Irene B. and Joseph R. Libby, Enfield, Connecticut.

Am. Can. Ch. Valentine's Prince Rudolph is by Ch. Montravia Jazz M'Tazz ex Ch. Dove-Cote's Valentine Heidi. Owned by Irene B. and James R. Libby.

Can. Am. Ch. Cadott's Kasper the Ghost, by Can. Am. Ch. Cadott's Edwin Gregory Snoluck ex Ch. Cadott's Premacelica of Lucky. Owner, Harriett Cadott.

Can. Ch. Cadott's Grand Marquis owned by Harriet Cadott, Glenburnie, Ontario.

Winning Best of Breed at an important Specialty Show, *Am. and Can. Ch. Talewagons Trinity* is owned and bred by Shirley M. Baxter.

Ch. Talewagons Open Sesame is from Talewagon Kennels, Willowdale, Ontario.

and to his modern French background reflected in his beauty.

Canadian Bichons are exceptionally correct and beautiful dogs thanks to dedicated breeders who are working with care and enthusiasm to produce and present Bichons at their very finest. As our illustrations point out, their goals are being achieved. Also it is interesting that by now all parts of the Bichon world are contributing to Canadian quality. At present there are fabulous examples of the quality to be found in Europe, Australia, England and the United States being incorporated into Canadian breeding programs thanks to some very desirable importations who have been brought there for the betterment of the breed.

BICHON FRISE CLUB OF CANADA REVISED BREED STANDARD

Origin and Purpose

The Bichon Frise originated in the Canary Islands and was formerly called the Bichon Teneriffe after the largest of this group of islands. It has been bred as a companion dog because of its friendly and affectionate nature.

General Appearance

The Bichon Frise is a small, sturdy, white powder puff of a dog, its dark-eyed, intelligent expression, and

BIS Am. and Can. Ch. Sno Puff's Ami de Neigenuveaux **belongs to Florence Erwin, Mississauga. Ontario.**

plumed tail carried jauntily over the back, attest to its merry temperament and create an overall air of elegance and dignity.

This is a breed that has no gross or incapacitating exaggerations and therefore there is no inherent reason for lack of balance or unsound movement.

Any deviation from the ideal described in the standard should be penalized to the extent of the deviation. Structural faults common to all breeds are as undesirable in the Bichon Frise as in any other breed, even though such faults may not be specifically mentioned in the standard.

Temperament
Alert, gentle mannered, playful and affectionate. A cheerful attitude is the hallmark of the breed and one should settle for nothing less.

Size
Dogs and bitches 9.5" to 11.5" are to be given primary preference. Only where the comparative superiority of a specimen outside this range clearly justifies it should greater latitude be taken. In no case, however, should this latitude ever extend over 12" or under 9". The minimum limits do not apply to puppies.

Coat and Colour
The texture of the coat is of utmost importance. The undercoat is soft and dense, the outercoat of a coarser and curlier texture. The combination of the two gives a soft but substantial feel to the touch which is similar to plush or velvet and when patted, springs back.

Can., Monaco and Int. Ch. Ami's Rick de Neigenuveaux in July 1990 after returning from France. Born on December 15, 1985, this exquisite son of BIS Am., Can. Ch. Snoupuff's Ami de Neigenuveaux was bred and is owned by Florence Erwin, Mississauga, Ontario. He was the first Canadian Bichon ever sent to France to be used in breeding programs.

Ch. Kenningway's Mercedes Benz is an outstanding Canadian winner and sire. This son of Ch. Vale Park the Challenger ex Am. Can. Ch. Vale Park Craigdale Classic is not only himself a leading winner, but went on to produce Canada's Top Winning Bichon Frise for 1989, Ch. Kenningway's Hairy Baby. Kenningway's Bichons are owned by Kendra James, Regina, Saskatchewan.

The coat is trimmed to reveal the natural outline of the body. It is rounded off from any direction and never cut so short as to create an overly trimmed or squared off appearance. The furnishings of the head, beard, moustache, arch of neck, ears and tail are left longer. The longer head hair is trimmed to create an overall rounded impression. The topline is trimmed to appear level. The coat is long enough to maintain the powder puff look which is characteristic of the breed, and when bathed, brushed and trimmed, the coat stands off the body, creating an overall powder puff appearance. A wiry coat is not desirable. A limp silky coat that lies down, or a lack of undercoat are very serious faults.

The colour is white. There may be shadings of buff, cream or apricot around the ears or on the body. Any colour in excess of 10% of the entire coat of a mature specimen is a fault and should be penalized, but colour of the accepted shadings should not be faulted in puppies.

Head
(a) Skull
The skull is slightly rounded, allowing for a round and forward looking eye. The skull should be broad, not coarse, covered with a topknot of hair giving it a rounded appearance.
(b) Muzzle
A properly balanced head is three parts muzzle to five parts skull. This is measured from the nose to the stop and from the stop to the occiput. The stop is slightly accentuated. A line drawn between the outside corners of the eyes and to the nose will create a near equilateral triangle. There is a slight degree of chiseling under the eyes, but not so much as to result in a weak or snipey foreface. The lower jaw is strong.
(c) Nose
The nose is prominent and always black.

(d) Mouth

Lips are black, fine, never drooping. Bite is scissors. A bite which is undershot or overshot should be penalized. A crooked or out of line tooth is permissible, however missing teeth are to be severely faulted.

(e) Eyes

Eyes are round, black or dark brown and are set in the skull to look directly forward. An overly large or bulging eye is a fault as is an almond shaped, obliquely set eye. Halos, the black or very dark brown skin surrounding the eyes, are necessary as they accentuate the eye and enhance expression. The eye rims themselves must be black. Broken pigment, or total absence of pigment on the eye rims produces a blank and staring expression, which is a definite fault. Eyes of any colour other than black or dark brown is a very serious fault and must be severely penalized.

(f) Ears

The ears are dropped and covered with long, flowing hair. When extended towards the nose, the leathers reach approximately halfway the length of the muzzle. They are set on slightly higher than eye level and rather forward on the skull so

Can. Ch. Azara Sir Auscan was imported from Australia to Canada from Azara Kennels by Merville and Marguerite Landry at Fran Bel Bichons in Beresford, New Brunswick. Born in September 1985, this lovely dog is a son of Aust. Ch. Jazz de la Buthiere of Leijazulip ex Keleb Snuggle Dumplin.

that when the dog is alert they frame the face.

Neck

The arched neck is long and carried proudly behind an erect head. It blends smoothly into the shoulders. The length of neck from occiput to withers is approximately one-third the distance from forechest to buttocks.

Forequarters

(a)   Shoulder

The shoulder blade, upper arm and forearm are approximately equal in length. The shoulders are laid back to somewhat near a forty-five degree angle.

(b)   Upper Arm

The upper arm extends well back so that elbow is placed directly below the withers when viewed from the side. The elbows are held close to the body.

(c)   Lower Arm

Legs are of medium bone; straight, with no bow or curve in the forearm or wrist.

(d) Pasterns

The pasterns slope slightly from the vertical. The dewclaws may be removed.

(e) Feet

The feet are tight and round, resembling those of a cat and point directly forward, turning neither in nor out. Pads are black. Nails are kept short.

Body

The body from the forwardmost part of the chest to the point of rump is 25% longer than the height at the withers. The body from the withers to lowest point of the chest represents half the distance from withers to ground. The back from the withers to the set of tail is slightly shorter than the dog is tall.

(a) Topline

The topline is level except for a slight, muscular arch over the loin.

(b) Chest

The chest is well developed and wide enough to allow free and unrestricted movement of the front legs. The lowest point of the chest extends at least to the elbow. The forechest is well pronounced and protrudes slightly forward of the point of shoulder. The rib cage is moderately sprung and extends back to a short and muscular loin.

(c) Abdomen

The abdomen is well muscled, not flabby, with a moderate tuck-up.

(d) Loin

The loin is short and muscular

(e) Croup

There is a slight, muscular arch over the loin. The croup is level.

Hindquarters

(a) Hipbone

Flat, not protruding,

Above: *Can. Ch. Craigdale Gypsy Rondo*, bred and co-owned by Dale Hunter. Below: Owned by Dale Hunter and Garda Johnstone, this is *Ch. Craigdale Carda Ms. Lil.*

slightly muscular.

(b) Upper Thigh/Lower Thigh

The upper and lower thighs are nearly equal in length, meeting at the stifle bend.

(c) Hocks

The leg from hock joint to foot pad is perpendicular to the ground.

(d) Stifle Bend

The stifle joint is well bent.

(e) Feet

Paws are tight and round with black, thick pads. The dewclaws may be removed.

Tail

The tail is well plumed, set on level with the topline and curved gracefully over the back in line with the spine so that the hair of the tail rests on the back. Carried in this way and extended forward towards the head it reaches at least halfway to the withers. A low tail set, a tail carried perpendicular to the back or a tail which droops behind is to be penalized. A corkscrew tail is a very serious fault.

Gait

Movement at a trot is free, precise and effortless. In profile the forelegs and hind legs extend equally with an easy reach and drive that maintains a steady topline. When

Am. Can. Ch. Bichonhaven's Casanova attained his Canadian Championship while still a puppy. He completed his American title when he took Winners Dog at the National Specialty in Texas. Born in February 1988, a son of Ch. Bichonhavens Q-Tip ex Bichonhavens Lady Luck, he has several champions to his credit. Bred and owned by Angela Baldwin, Mansfield, Ontario.

Can. and Am. Ch. Cadott's Gregory Snoluck was born in July 1987, sired by Can. Ch. Snopuff's Goodluck Bear ex Can. Ch. Trevor's Lucky Touch of Class. Owned by Harriet Cadott, Glenburnie, Ontario.

moving, the head and neck remain somewhat erect and as speed increases there is a very slight convergence of legs toward the centre line. Moving away, the hindquarters travel with moderate width between them and the foot pads can be seen. Coming and going, movement is precise and true.

Faults

Cowhocks; incorrect head proportions; poor pigmentation; protruding or almond shaped eyes; undershot or overshot bite; missing teeth; incorrect body proportions; incorrect tail set or carriage; overly trimmed coat on adults or puppies which does not portray a powder puff appearance; aggressive or shy behaviour.

Disqualifications

Over 12" or under 9"; yellow eyes; black hair in the coat; pink eye rims and/or nose; showing aggression by biting or snapping.

Cadott's Sonata Snowfall, owned by Barbara Elizabeth Wustafeld, Toronto, and bred by Harriet Cadott.

Am. and Can. Ch. Enjoue Monsieur Lacrosse at age 4 weeks. Owners, Ed and Anne Jones, Charles City, Virginia.

Am. Can. Ch. Valentine's Scoot Sammy owned by Irene B. and Joseph R. Libby, Enfield, Connecticut.

Yoannewyn's Dream of Aspinrock, owned by Debbie McFarlane and Anne Yocum, Bragg Creek, Alberta, who also bred this adorable puppy.

Cadott's Chelsey Kingsworth in the Butterworth family portrait. Owned by Lynn Butterworth, Peterborough, Ontario.

Neigenuveaux Bichon puppies from the kennels of Florence Erwin, Mississauga, Ontario.

Can. Ch. Delongte's Aurora Bella is owned by Mrs. Marion Stockman of Aurora, Ontario. She is a daughter of Ch. Darkel's Artic Star, her pedigree tracing back to such noted Bichons as Ch. Vogelflight's Choir Master and Beau Monde The Actor.

Am. Can. Ch. Cullford B-Major relaxes with his owner/handler Angela Baldwin of Mansfield, Ontario.

Ch. Aldo's Abba owner-bred by Doug Buckingham and Alda White.

Ch. Dauphine De Fran Bel owned by Norma Dirszowsky.

Am. Can. Ch. Crockerly Moon Olé Toreador. Photo courtesy of Dale Hunter.

Am. Can. Ch. Rondia's Bright Eyes-Bushy Tail owned by Norma Dirszowsky.

Am. Can. Ch. Windstars Mr. Charisma owned by E. Kellerman and J. Gueli.

Am. Can. Ch. Kibbatts Craigdale Joy owned by D. Hunter and P. Mason.

Winners Dog at the Bichon Frise Club of America National Specialty, *Bichonhavens Casanova* completed his title for Canadian Champion. This beautiful Bichon is owned and was bred by Angela Baldwin, Mansfield, Ontario.

The beautiful *Am. Can. Ch. Beau Monde Works D'Arte Witty* with her owner Wendy Kellerman. Bred by Bobby Sue McKenley, this bitch is the All Time #8 Top Producing Dam in the breed.

Bichons in Australia

Bichons have become extremely popular and successful in Australia following their start there during 1976, when Bichon fever seemed at a high pitch around the world. Their progress undoubtedly is based both on the intelligence of the breeders and on the availability of the finest American and British bloodlines. From the very beginning Australian breeders have had the cream of the crop with which to work and the instinct to do it right.

Australia and Bichons discovered one another as a result of noted hound folks Harry and Margaret McKenzie-Beggs, owners of splendid Afghan Hounds and Salukis, who decided that the time had come for them to seek a smaller breed. Their search for one they would like, took them to England and the Leander Kennels of John and Wendy Streatfield. Leander is world-famous for their Poodles, but the Streatfields discovered a new canine love—the adorable small white dog known as the Bichon Frise. The McKenzie-Beggs's almost instantly succumbed to the charms of the Bichons they saw at Leander, so they promptly made the purchase of their first. Their choice was Am. Ch. Beau Monde the Snowdrift of Leander, by the USA Top Show Dog and Top Producer, Am. Ch. Chaminade Mr. Beau Monde and Works D'Arte Miro Chaminade.

Snowdrift was an instant success in Australia. As might have been expected, very shortly more well-bred and handsome Bichons followed from England on "down under."

This was only the beginning! These early dogs who came behind Snowdrift to the McKenzie-Beggs's brought with them still more of California's most prized breeding, of which a nucleus was quickly formed that was to become totally successful. Right behind Snowdrift in the mid-1970s came Carlise Cicero of Tresilva, a son of the first two Bichons to arrive in Great Britain, Rava's Reak Valor of Reenroy, and Jennie Vive de Carlise. Cicero was sold to Mrs. Jackie Ransom, then later by her to Australia where he became a champion and did his bit as a producer.

Am. Ch. C and D's Beau Monde Sunflower of Leander, who had been sired by Mr. Beau Monde

ex Am. C and D 's Countess Becky was among these earliest arrivals; as was Aust. Ch. Beau Monde the Dove of Leander, by Am. Ch. C and D's Count Kristopher ex Am. Ch. Beau Monde The Vamp. There is no denying Mr. and Mrs. McKenzie-Beggs are credited as having introduced a fast rising breed to Australia when they brought the first one there!

Approximately two dozen imports quickly represented Leander and the American breeders in Australia. Soon a great many Australian fanciers were following the importation route. Among them, note should be made of two ladies, Dianne Crosby-Brown and France Wilson, owners of Ancrowns Kennels and Planhaven Kennels, respectively. Their purchases consisted of four. The first pair, Leander Snow Scout and Leander Snow Bubbles, were sired by Am. Aust. Ch. Beau Monde The Snowdrift of

Ch Reenroy's Ami du Kilkanny with her grand-daughter, *Works D'Artes Chaminade* who became the dam of the first Bichon Champion in Australia. Photo by Missy Yuhl.

Leander ex Am. Aust. Ch. C and D's Beau Monde Sunflower of Leander. The other two in this group were Leander Snow Cap and Snow Girl, they sired by Am. Ch. C and D 's Beau Monde Blizzard ex Val Va Don's Chantee of Leander.

It was Snow Cap and Bubbles who gave Australia the first litter of Bichons Frises born there. Am. Aust. Ch. C and D's Beau Monde Sunflower of Leander, an extremely notable producer of quality, also came eventually to Australia.

Rudi Van Voorst has been most helpful with information and photographs of dogs who have strongly influenced the progress of Bichons in Australia. Rudi and Frank

Vallely are owners of the now world-famous Azara Kennels in Victoria. They became fans and owners of the breed through their interest and attraction to a photograph in a dog magazine of a Bichon owned by Mrs. Celeste Fleishman in the United States. This Bichon was Am. Ch. Stardom's Niki of Staramour, a homebred from Celeste's Staramour Kennels in Pennsylvania, and of course Rudi and Frank could hardly wait to have one of their own! A wish that by now has been fulfilled time and time again, as Azara has become one of the strongholds for real quality in the breed. Am. Aust. Ch. Leander Snow Mittens came there in 1974, by Leander Snow Venture ex Am. Aust. Ch. C and D's Beau Monde Sunflower of Leander, mentioned above for her fine producing record, added substantially to that following her arrival in Australia. Rudi has helped enormously in my collecting of information, opinions and photographs for this book. I shall forever be appreciative!

A Bichon who really took his world by storm was Aust. Ch. Jazz de la Buthiere of Leijazulip, generally described as "Australia's most influential import." A Son

Aust. Ch. Leander Snow Mittens, by Leander Snow Venture ex Am. and Aust. Ch. C. and D.'s Beau Monde Sun Flower. She is the dam of 12 champions. Owned by Azara Bichons, Ivanhoe, Victoria.

Top: *Aust. Ch. Jazz de La Buthiere of Leijazulip* owned by Azara Kennels in Australia. Bottom: *Aust. Ch. Azara Bijan* owned by Azara Bichons, Ivanhoe, Victoria.

of Int. Ch. If de la Buthiere ex French Ch. Vanda de la Buthiere, this Jazz was purchased from Mrs. Vera Goold in England, and it was definitely quite a coup to obtain this marvelous winner of 20 times Best in Show and sire of 31 champions, surely making a record to admire, which we believe still stands.

When Azara makes a decision, action is taken promptly. In this case, the concentration has been on quality bitches there; but then when it seemed time to start adding some admirable males, Jazz became only a starter. Quickly he was followed by Aust., French, German,

Right: *Can. Ch. Azara Romy* sired by Aust. Ch. Nagamuzi Mr. Frosty of Zudiki ex Aust. Ch. Leijazulip Angelique. Bred by Frank Valley and Rudi Van Voorst. Romy is pictured here completeing his Canadian title with his owner/handler Mr. Merville Landry. Below: *Aust. Ch. Leijazulip Angelique*, a daughter of Leilah de La Buthiere of Leijazulip owned by Azara Bichons, Ivanhoe, Victoria.

Swedish and Int. Ch. Looping de la Buthiere, by Int. Ch. If de la Buthiere ex Int. Ch. Vania de Villa Sainval, imported direct from Mme. Desfarge from France. Plus, a third male, Aust. Ch. Nagazumi Mr. Frosty of Zudiki purchased from Jo Brown Emerson in England. Then came the second outstanding purchase of a bitch, Aust. Ch. Leijazulip Angelique, (by Jazz de la Buthiere ex Leilah de la Buthiere of Leijazulip), who went on to become a Top Producer dam of 14 champions. A dog and a bitch from Judy Fausset of Kaleb Kennels in the U.S. completed the foundation dogs on which Azara was created.

Our wonderful Australian photos in this book will show you many of the spectacular, excellent and striking Bichons who have descended from this source! You will see, with

admiration, Aust. Ch. Azara Le President and three bitches; Aust. Ch. Azara Petit Fleur, Aust. Ch. Azare MaBelle and Aust. Ch. Azare Desiree, who have accomplished big things in the ring, including the winning of 21 Bests in Show plus producing over a dozen champions. Needless to say, these Bichons have provided foundation for various other successful breeders in Australia and New Zealand. There is also another Bichon named Jazz, this one English and Aust. Ch. Leijazulip Jazz de Zudiki, son of Int. Ch. Leijazulip Guillaume ex Ninon de la Buthiere, who, imported by Wendy and John Hutchinson of Victoria, was the first English Bichon Champion to come to Australia. Also

This little Bichon became the first Australian-bred member of his breed to come to America and gain championship status. *Am. Ch. Azara King Shalmaneser*, by Ch. Nagazumi Mr. Frosty of Zudiki ex Ch. Leijazulip Angelique was sent to Mr. Mike Nagy in New Jersey by Azara Bichons, Ivanhoe, Victoria.

they have enjoyed lots of spectacular winning and champion progeny from their two Azara-bred daughters of Jazz de la Buthiere.

This author feels that the Australian people are to be highly commended on the high quality of their dogs. Also they are well groomed and well presented, which is a "must" wherever the competition becomes keen and really close between the various dogs.

Australia's top Bichon for 1980, 1981 and 1982, *Ch. Azara's Petite Fleur* relaxes in the garden at home with a friend. In addition to all her own many successes in the ring, Petite Fleur is the dam of six noted champions.

Aust. Ch. Azara Le Presidente who is owned by Mrs. Betty Brown in Australia is Australia's Top Australian-bred Best in Show winning Bichon. Bred by Azara Bichons Ivanhoe, Victoria.

The beautiful head and expression of *Aus. Ch. Alhaja Daniel Le Beau.* Owned, groomed and handled by Caroline Lile for breeder/owner Mr. D. Stone. This lovely dog from New South Wales is by Ch. Zettamy Ice Master ex Mexicath Michelle. Included among his ring successes are his having 11 times been awarded Best Exhibit in Show, and in 1988, 1990, and 1991 he was winner of the Bichon Frise Club of New South Wales "Dog of the Year."

Right: A notable winner in Australia, this is *Aust. Ch. Chismene Isabella.* Owned by Mrs. J. Jeffrey, Sydney.

Lower left: Aust. Ch. Zipadedoda Michlas Magic, owned by Mrs. J. Jeffrey, Sydney. Lower right: *Aust. Ch. Peterina Tres Jacques,* owned by Mrs. J. Jeffrey, Sydney.

Upper left:
Aust. Ch.
Zettamay
Certain
Fame,
owned by C.
Van Beek,
Dee Why,
New South
Wales.
Upper right:
Australian
Ch. Alhaja
La Belle
Helene,
owned by,
Caroline Lill,
Wahroonga,
New South
Wales.

Left: Azara
Carolinee,
owned by
Azara
Bichons, R.
Van Voorst
and F.C.
Valley,
Ivanhoe,
Victoria.

Am. Ch. Azara Christina, by Ch. Nagazumi Mr. Frosty of Zudiki ex Keleb Snuggle Dumplin, was bred by Azara Bichons in Australia and is owned by Miss Sally Mitchell, Sacramento, California.

Can. Ch. Azara Sir Auscan owned by Mr. and Mrs. Merville Landry. Sir Auscan was bred by Frank Valley and Rudi Van Voorst in Australia, sired by Aust. Ch. Jazz de la Buthiere ex Kaleb Snuggle Dumplin.

Cannondale Dom Perignone and *Cannondale Moete Chanson*, bred and owned by Miss P.Page, Mandaley Cattai, New South Wales.

Bichons in New Zealand

Mr. and Mrs. Allan Crooks, owners of Silverlea kennels at Christchurch, are the folks who introduced the Bichon Frise in New Zealand. Again it was a published photograph that attracted their attention to the adorable little white dogs. In this case the subject was the first AKC all-breed Best in Show winner, Ch. Chaminade Syncopation owned by Mrs. William Tabler of New York. One look at Syncopation's picture and the decision had been made that this breed definitely was for them.

In 1976, Betty Miryless was contacted in England and the purchase made of a male Bichon, a puppy dog with the name Beaupres Casanova out of a bitch named Carlise Canny Caprice of Beaupres. His arrival in New Zealand was in August, 1977. He was destined to become New Zealand's first Bichon Champion.

So delighted were Mr. and Mrs. Crooks with their new breed and new dog that they soon were back in touch with Mrs. Miryless regarding the purchase of a bitch to breed to Casanova. This is when they imported Beaupres Astrid, who on November 7, 1978 presented the Crooks with the first litter of Bichons whelped in New Zealand. Two of these puppies, Mystic Miss of Silverlea and Andre of Silverlea, became the first New Zealand-born champions.

Toward the end of the 1970s there was tremendous Bichon activity in both the North Island and the South Island. The first became the first import brought to the North Island, Leander Snow Jingle, who came to Elsie Rennie. Leander Snow Petal and Leander Snow Print did likewise. Then, later on, came Beau Monde White Wine, by the great Ch. Chaminade Mr. Beau Monde, who was shipped to England after being bred to Am. Ch. Beau Monde the Huckster.

Aust. and N.Z. Ch. Kynismar Rare Chance, an import from the UK, belongs to Jean Fife in New Zealand.

Bichons in Europe

The author acknowledges Bichon Frise owners in Europe who have provided pictures for this book.

Skovfryd Snow Rosie was Best of Breed at the World Show in 1992. Owned by Karina Christofhersen, Bastemosevej, Tranekaer, Denmark. Snow Rosie is by Azura Lord Jim ex Beau Monde Top Class.

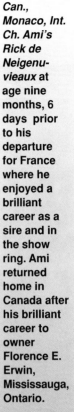

Can., Monaco, Int. Ch. Ami's Rick de Neigenu-vieaux at age nine months, 6 days prior to his departure for France where he enjoyed a brilliant career as a sire and in the show ring. Ami returned home in Canada after his brilliant career to owner Florence E. Erwin, Mississauga, Ontario.

Dutch, Ger., Bel., Int. Ch. Azara Emilia, at Liege in Belgium winning the Best in Show attained over a field of 2,500 competitors. Bred in Australia by the Azara Bichons, Emilia is owned by the noted International judge Mrs. C. Koudys, Holland.

Photographed by her owner, V.J. Probst in Switzerland, this is *Int. Ch. Sisside de La Buthiere*. Note the coat, face, and size. She is groomed in the French way—the coat longer than in the United States.

Denmark's noted multiple Best in Show winning Bichon, *DKCh, SFCh, Int. Ch. Beau Monde Cameo Callboy* is owned by G. Nymann and H. Rusk, Fjenneslev. Callboy had a high rating as #8 Dog of the Year among all breeds for 1990.

Azzjazz the Danish Blue, an outstanding Bichon from Kennel Skovfryd, owned by Karina Christopher-sen, Bastemo-sevej, Tranekaer, Denmark. This little dog was the World Winner at Copenhagen in 1989.

This is *Azara Adairing* at two months of age, owned by Mrs. V.J. Probst in Switzerland. Sired by Chazz de La Buthiere ex Keleb Snuggle Dumplin.

A dog of fame and quality, this is *DKCh, SFCh, Int. Ch. Beau Monde Cameo Callboy* owned by G. Nymann and H. Rusk, Fjenneslev, Denmark. Callboy was the top winning Bichon Frise in Denmark during 1989, 1990 and 1991.

Top left: *Int. Ch. Kynismar Bugsy Malone*, bred by Mrs. Aikins in England, is being posed by Mrs. Stray in Norway. Top right: *Nor., Sw., Fin., Int. Ch. Azara Petite Carmen*, by Ch. Jazz de La Buthiere of Leijozulip ex Ch. Leijozulip Angelique. Bred by Australia's Azara Kennels, Carmen is owned by Mrs. Berit Nilsen. She was the Top Bichon in Norway in 1985 and 1986 and top Bichon bitch in 1984. Bottom: *Int. Ch. Kynismar Winterlude Angel* was Norway's top winning Bichon for 1990. Sired by Billy The Kid ex Kynismar Coco Chanel, Angel was bred by Mr. M. Aikins and is owned by Mrs. E. Stray.

Top: Here are two of the French International Champions sired by the great Ami's Rick. They are *Int. Ch. Douchka de La Manoir* owned by Mrs. Buissonnets, and *Fr. Int. Ch. Charly de Le Manoir des Buissonnets*. Photo courtesy of Ami's Canadian breeder/owner, Florence E. Erwin. Bottom: Two lovely Bichons from France, both of them National and World International Champions, are highly representative of the quality Bichon produced at Buthiere Kennels. These are *Pablo de La Buthiere*, who was winner of these titles for 1981; and *Orgon de La Buthiere*, who had gained them in 1980.

Azara Adairing, and *Int. Ch. Sisi de La Buthiere* owned by Mrs. V.J. Probst in France. They were sired respectively by Ch. Jazz and Ch. Pablo.

Why a Bichon?

Have you ever noticed the very special pride and satisfaction of dog owners you've just met as they tell you, that "*My* dog is a *Bichon*"? The smiles on the faces of these people speak for themselves. Here we have a Bichon fancier delighted to have selected that breed and anxious to share with the world how great a dog it is proving to be.

Bichons affect people that way. To this discriminating group they have indeed found a very special dog, and few of them (if any at all) ever change their opinion over the years.

Bichons do have lots to offer. From their distinctive good looks to

their obvious sturdiness; their alert, merry expression; and the friendly wagging tail make one just *know* that this is an interesting, worthy little fellow. Plus, the Bichon is easy and fun to live with, will not irritate one's allergies, and will love your entire household throughout his long lifetime, which usually runs to the middle teens.

They are thoroughly satisfactory dogs. They are what I like to speak of as "handy home size" in that, despite many big dog characteristics, they are themselves small, measuring in at 9½ to 11½ inches tall at the withers. But they are hardier than many dogs that size.

A Bichon is a sweet, loving and affectionate dog. He is full of fun and mischief, playful, agreeable with other pets, and great with children, seeming to have endless enthusiasm for their games. When you bring in a new puppy, though, please remember that children can be thoughtlessly rough in playing with puppies; so please have it clearly agreed upon that the puppy is a live friend, *not* a toy, and that therefore he

These two exciting Bichons are "Maka," *Chaminade Improvisation* and "Kerri," *Ch. Chaminade Jugue*. Both belong to Terry and Michael Ranin of Los Angeles. Photo courtesy of Barbara Stubbs.

must *not* be hurt, nor injured, nor frightened. Be sure about your children's friends, too, that they do not take advantage of the puppy or dog with a less than gentle touch.

Bichons love to be dressed up, as children adore doing with their pets who usually object. The Bichon, though, never objects. I cannot help feeling that this takes them back to their circus days and the costumes they then used in their routines!

The keen alertness of your Bichon makes him a competent and useful watchdog. He will guard your home and property with energy, and be quick to sound an alarm should, to him, a suspicious situation arise, and make exactly the noisy fuss most feared by prowlers, would-be burglars, or others up to no good. We are all aware that the major usefulness of a watchdog is his spreading of the news that something strange is happening and he is not one to just sit quietly and watch. To not be noticed or discovered is obviously an important matter through the eyes of a burglar, so an upset and excited dog prompts the intruder to

Ch. Proud Land's Apache Kid at five months old sharing in Halloween festivities. He is a beloved family pet as well as a successful show winner owned by John and Sigma Toth, Pennsylvania.

Cadott's Suzie Sunshine at ten months of age. Bred and owned by Ursala Haslhofer, Hamilton, Ontario.

Cadott's Aladdin celebrates his birthday. Owners, Jim and Thelma Bergendahl, Kingston, Ontario.

take off for unprotected and thus quiet, more workable places. It has always been my opinion that small dogs as watchdogs are great. One does not really need a "man eater" for this purpose; just one with a lot of energy and a loud voice who will stick with it until the "caller" has become unnerved and taken off elsewhere.

Where your Bichon lives is of little concern to him, so long as you are there. Owing to his ideal size, he fits in well wherever, be it in the city or the country. He prefers being a house dog to living in a kennel. His favorite spot is curled up on your lap or beside you on the couch.

A tremendous asset to Bichon owners is the fact

that these little dogs do not shed, and thus are hypoallergenic. What a boon for all the dog lovers who for years thought they could not have the pleasure of a dog due to their own allergies! If you are among those, by all means try a Bichon. It's just that simple. I know of numerous happy Bichon owners who for years felt that they could never enjoy the pleasure of a canine companion of their own, but found that with this breed they *could.*

In case you are anxious to do it but at the same time worried it might not work out, make arrangements to spend an

afternoon at a Bichon kennel or a home where they have one or more as pets, and see if you feel any ill effects. I will bet *no.* Do be sure that dogs of no other breed are also kept there, nor a cat, as then you would not be giving it a fair trial.

Non-shedding dogs are marvelous not only for

allergy reasons, but also for maintenance. With a Bichon, there is no shed-out dog hair all over your clothes, furniture, and rugs, which must ordinarily be gone through with other dogs during "shedding season" once or twice a year. Just think of the work saved in hair-removal from all those fabrics!

Nothing is entirely without its price, as we are all aware. In this case that price is that dogs with non-shedding coats are more inclined to mat. It is not difficult to handle that, however. All it takes is frequent brushing, perhaps even on a daily basis. If, however, you permit mats to get started then it *does* become a problem as they, once formed, are tedious and difficult. Sometimes they must be cut away with

Bichon pets owned by Mrs. B. Yann, Australia, enjoying water sports.

Ch.Camelot's Brassy Nickel, CDX, sunglasses in place, waits to see what will turn up. Owned by Mrs. Pam Goldman, New Jersey.

frequent baths in order to be at their sparkling best. But most important of all is keeping the coats brushed out and free of mats!

Bichons get on well with other animals and pets in the household just as they do with people. Thus I think the best of all ways in which to enhance your enjoyment of your dog is to get a *second* Bichon. They will amuse one another and you with their games and antics, playing happily together; and your absence from home will not leave your little friend feeling lonely as he will have another of his own kind for company. It is my personal opinion that an only dog in even the most loving of homes is somehow a sad little dog, and that in so sociable a breed it is a pity *not* to have two sharing their lives together.

Being what I like to speak of as "handy home size," two are almost no more work than one, especially as you can even walk them on leads together. Do seriously consider this, for it truly *would* "double your pleasure."

There is nothing nervous about a Bichon. They are calm and steady, filled with enthusiasm and good humor and have zest for life and its pleasures.

Good pals Taylor Goldman and *Indiana Joan*. Photo courtesy of Pam Goldman, Livingston, New Jersey.

blunt scissors, then given time to fill in again to keep your little powder puff coat smooth, full, and beautiful. There is lots about coat care and grooming in this book, so you will find sound advice to follow in order to make the most of your Bichon's well dressed appearance.

Remember, too, that white dogs need fairly

The famous *Ch. Chaminade Syncopation*, by Petit Galant de St. George ex Ch. Chaminade Sonata, was bred by pioneer fanciers Richard Beauchamp and Barbara Stubbs. "Snidely" was the first Bichon Frise ever to win Best in Show at an AKC all- breed dog show. Owned by Mrs. William B. Tabler and handled by Ted Young, Jr., Snidely was the Top Winning Bichon of 1973, 1974 and 1975. Photo courtesy of *Kennel Review*.

The Purchase of the Bichon

Careful consideration should be given to what breed of dog you wish to own prior to your purchase of one. If several breeds are attractive to you, and you are undecided as to which you prefer, learn all you can about the characteristics of each before making your decision. As you do so, you are thus preparing yourself to make an intelligent choice; and this is very important when buying a dog who will be, with reasonable luck, a member of your household for at least a dozen years or more. Obviously, since you are reading this book, you have decided on the breed—so now all that remains is to make a good choice.

It is never wise to just rush out and buy the first cute puppy who catches your eye. Whether you wish a dog to show, one with whom to compete in obedience, or one as a family dog purely for his (or her) companionship, the more time and thought you invest as you plan the purchase, the more likely you are to meet with complete satisfaction. The background and early care behind your pet will reflect in the dog's future health and temperament. Even if you are planning the purchase purely as a pet, with no thoughts of showing or breeding in the dog's or puppy's future, it is

essential that, if the dog is to enjoy a trouble-free future, you assure yourself of a healthy, properly raised puppy or adult from sturdy, well-bred stock.

Throughout the pages of this book you will find the names and locations of many well-known and well-established kennels in various areas. Other sources of information are the American Kennel Club (51 Madison Avenue, New York, New York 10010) and the Kennel Club (1 Clarges Street, Piccadilly, London, W1Y 8AB) from whom you can obtain a list of recognized breeders in the vicinity of your home. If

These young charmers are Bichon Frise puppies owned by Patricia Dale Hunter, North Vancouver, British Columbia.

you plan to have your dog campaigned by a professional handler, by all means let the handler help you locate and select a good dog. Through their numerous clients, handlers have access to a variety of interesting show prospects; and the usual arrangement is that the handler re-sells the dog to you for what his cost has been, with the agreement that the dog be campaigned for you by him

with bright eyes and intelligent expression and who is friendly and alert; avoid puppies who are hyperactive, dull, or listless. The coat should be clean and thick, with no sign of parasites. The premises on which he was raised should look (and smell) clean and be tidy, making it obvious that the puppies and their surroundings are in capable hands. Should the

throughout the dog's career. It is most strongly recommended that prospective purchasers follow these suggestions, as you thus will be better able to locate and select a satisfactory puppy or dog.

Your first step in searching for your puppy is to make appointments at kennels specializing in your breed, where you can visit and inspect the dogs, both those available for sale and the kennel's basic breeding stock. You are looking for an active, sturdy puppy

Bichon Frise kennels be sparse in your area or not have what you consider attractive, do not hesitate to contact others at a distance and purchase from them if they seem better able to supply a puppy or dog who will please you—*so long as it is a recognized breeding kennel of that breed.* Shipping dogs is a regular practice nowadays, with comparatively few problems when one considers the number of dogs shipped each year. A reputable, well-known breeder wants the customer to be satisfied; thus, he will represent the puppy fairly. Should you not be pleased with the puppy upon arrival, a breeder, such as described, will almost certainly permit its return. A conscientious breeder takes real interest and concern in the welfare of the dogs he or she causes to be brought into the world. Such a breeder also is proud of a reputation for integrity. Thus on two counts, for the sake of the dog's future and the breeder's reputation, to such a person a *satisfied* customer takes precedence over a sale at any cost.

If your puppy is to be a pet or "family dog," the earlier the age at which it joins your household the better. Puppies are weaned and ready to start out on their own, under the care of a sensible new owner, at about six weeks old; and if you take a young one, it is often easier to train it to the routine of your household and to your requirements of it than is the case with an older dog which, even though still technically a puppy, may have already started habits you will find difficult to change. The younger puppy is usually less costly, too, as it stands to reason the breeder will not have as much expense invested in it. Obviously, a puppy that has been raised to five or six months old represents more in care and cash expenditure on the

Two outstanding young Bichons owned by Michael and Toni Ambrosia, New Jersey. Daisy and Maximillion are by Ch. M. and A.'s Count D'Amour ex Sumarco's Aphrodite.

Extremely promising Bichon puppies at six-weeks of age, owned by Ed and Anne Jones, Virginia.

breed of which they were supposedly members was barely recognizable. So one cannot always judge a puppy by price alone. Common sense must guide a prospective purchaser, plus the selection of a *reliable,* well-recommended dealer whom you know to have well-satisfied customers or, best of all, a specialized breeder. You will probably find the fairest pricing at the kennel of a breeder. Such a person, experienced with the breed in general and with his or her own stock in particular, through extensive association with these dogs, has watched enough of them mature to have obviously learned to assess quite accurately each puppy's potential— something impossible where such background is non-existent.

breeder's part than one sold earlier; therefore he should be, and generally is, priced accordingly.

There is an enormous amount of truth in the statement that "bargain" puppies seldom turn out to be that. A "cheap" puppy, raised purely for sale and profit, can and often does lead to great heartbreak, including problems and veterinarian's bills which can add up to many times the initial cost of a properly reared dog. On the other hand, just because a puppy is expensive does not assure one that it is healthy and well reared. There have been numerous cases where unscrupulous dealers have sold, for several hundred dollars, puppies that were sickly, in poor condition, and such poor specimens that the

One more word on the subject of pets. Bitches make a fine choice for this purpose as they are usually quieter and more gentle than the males, easier to house train, more affectionate, and less inclined to roam. If you do select a bitch and have no intention of breeding or showing her, by all means have her spayed, for your sake and for hers. The advantages to the owner of a spayed bitch include avoiding the nuisance of "in season" periods which normally occur twice yearly—with the accompanying eager canine swains haunting your premises in an effort to get close to your female—plus the unavoidable messiness and spotting of furniture and rugs at this time, which can be annoying if occurring. It is recommended that all bitches eventually be spayed—even those used for show or breeding when their careers have ended—in order that they may enjoy a happier, healthier old age. Please take note, however, that a bitch who has been spayed (or an

These enchanting babies are Bichon puppies owned by Ginger Cerniglia.

she is a household companion in the habit of sharing your sofa or bed. As for the spayed bitch, she benefits as she grows older because this simple operation almost entirely eliminates the possibility of breast cancer ever altered dog) *cannot be shown at American Kennel Club or Kennel Club dog shows once this operation has been performed.* Be certain that you are *not* interested in showing her before taking this step.

Also, in selecting a pet,

Ch. Windstar'sThe Banjo Man, who as a pup here was already showing promise of a good career in the show ring. Bred and owned by Wendy Kellerman, he is a son of Ch. Windstar's Minstrel Singer and is among many noted winners owned by Robert A. Koeppel.

never underestimate the advantages of an older dog, perhaps a retired show dog or a bitch no longer needed for breeding, who may be available and quite reasonably priced by a breeder anxious to place such a dog in a loving home. These dogs are settled and can be a delight to own, as they make wonderful companions, especially in a household of adults where raising a puppy can sometimes be a trial.

Everything that has been said about careful selection of your pet puppy and its place of purchase applies, but with many further considerations, when you plan to buy a show dog or foundation stock for a future breeding program. Now is the time for an in-depth study of the breed,

starting with every word and every illustration in this book and all others you can find written on the subject. The Standard of the breed has now become your guide, and you must learn not only the words but also how to interpret them and how to apply them to actual dogs before you are ready to make an intelligent selection of a show dog.

If you are thinking in terms of a dog to show, obviously you must have learned about dog shows and must be in the habit of attending them. This is fine, but now your activity in this direction should be increased, with your attending every single dog show within a reasonable distance from your home. Much can be learned about a breed at ringside at these events. Talk with the breeders who are exhibiting. Study the dogs they are showing. Watch the judging with concentration, noting each decision made, and attempt to follow the reasoning by which the judge has reached it. Note carefully the attributes of the dogs who win and, for your later use, the manner in which each is presented. Close your ears to the ringside know-it-alls, usually novice owners of a dog or two and very new to the Fancy, who

have only derogatory remarks to make about all that is taking place unless they happen to win. This is the type of exhibitor who "comes and goes" through the Fancy and whose interest is usually of very short duration, owing to lack of knowledge and dissatisfaction caused by the failure to recognize the need to learn. You, as a fancier whom we hope will last and enjoy our sport over many future years, should develop independent thinking at this stage; you should learn to draw your own conclusions about the merits, or lack of them, seen before you in the ring and, thus, sharpen your own judgement in preparation for choosing wisely and well.

Note carefully which breeders campaign winning dogs—not just an occasional isolated good one, but consistent, homebred winners. It is from one of these people that you should select your own future "star."

If you are located in an area where dog shows take place only occasionally or where there are long travel distances involved, you will need to find another testing ground for your ability to select a worthy show dog. Possibly, there are some representative kennels raising this breed within a reasonable distance. If so, by all means ask permission of the owners to visit the kennels and do so when permission is granted. You may not necessarily buy then and

Twinley Bright Chrystal and Kynismar Boogie's Boy are sire and dam of this beautiful and healthy litter of seven puppies in 1987. Owner, Mrs. Pauline Block at Whitechurch, Hampshire, England.

Maribella Bichon litter at age seven-weeks belonging to Marion Stockman, By Can. Am. Ch. Cadott's Edwin Gregory Snoluck ex Can. Ch. Maribella Dream Girl.

there, as they may not have available what you are seeking that very day, but you will be able to see the type of dog being raised there and to discuss the dogs with the breeder. Every time you do this, you add to your knowledge. Should one of these kennels have dogs which especially appeal to you, perhaps you could reserve a show-prospect puppy from a coming litter. This is frequently done, and it is often worth waiting for a puppy, unless you have seen a dog with which you truly are greatly impressed and which is immediately available.

The purchase of a puppy has already been discussed. Obviously this same approach applies in a far greater degree when the purchase involved is a future show dog. The only place from which to purchase a show prospect is a breeder who raises show-type stock; otherwise, you are almost certainly doomed to disappointment as the puppy matures. Show and breeding kennels obviously cannot keep all of their fine young stock. An active breeder-exhibitor is, therefore, happy to place promising youngsters in the hands of people also interested in showing and winning with them, doing so at a fair price according to the quality and prospects of the dog involved. Here again, if no kennel in your immediate area has what you are seeking, do not hesitate to contact top breeders in other areas and to buy at long distance. Ask for pictures, pedigrees, and a complete description. Heed the breeder's advice and recommendations, after truthfully telling exactly what your expectations are for the dog you purchase. Do you want something with which to win just a few ribbons now and then? Do you want a dog who can complete his championship? Are you thinking of the real "big time" (i.e., seriously campaigning with Best of Breed, Group wins, and possibly even Best in Show as your eventual goal)?

Consider it all carefully in advance; then honestly discuss your plans with the breeder. You will be better satisfied with the results if you do this, as the breeder is then in the best position to help you choose the dog who is most likely to come through for you. A breeder selling a show dog is just as anxious as the buyer for the dog to succeed, and the breeder will represent the dog to you with truth and honesty. Also, this type of breeder does not lose interest the moment the sale has been made but, when necessary, will be right there to assist you with beneficial advice and suggestions based on years of experience.

As you make inquiries of at least several kennels, keep in mind that show-prospect puppies are less expensive than mature show dogs, the latter often costing close to four figures, and sometimes more. The reason for this is that, with a puppy, there is always an element of chance, the possibility of its developing unexpected faults as it matures or failing to develop the excellence and quality that earlier had seemed probable. There definitely is a risk factor in buying a show-prospect puppy. Sometimes all goes well, but occasionally the swan becomes an ugly duckling. Reflect on this as you consider available puppies and young adults. It just might be a good idea to go with a more mature, though more costly, dog if one you like is available.

When you buy a mature show dog, "what you see is what you get," and it is not likely to change beyond

A sleighful of Hooligan puppies sired by Can. Am. Ch. Wendar Fly the Flag ex Can. Ch. Hooligan's Dream Maker. These handsome babies bred and owned by Sandra Lyn Dawson, Okotoks, Alberta, Canada.

coat and condition, which are dependent on your care. Also advantageous for a novice owner is the fact that a mature dog of show quality almost certainly will have received show-ring training and probably match-show experience, which will make your earliest handling ventures much easier.

Frequently it is possible to purchase a beautiful dog who has completed championship but who, owing to similarity in bloodlines, is not needed for the breeder's future program. Here you have the opportunity of owning a champion, usually in the two-to-five-year-old range, which you can enjoy campaigning as a special (for Best of Breed competition) and which will be a settled, handsome dog for you and your family to enjoy with pride.

If you are planning foundation for a future kennel, concentrate on acquiring one or two really superior bitches. These need not be top show-quality, but they should represent your breed's finest producing bloodlines from a strain noted for producing quality, generation after generation. A proven matron who is already the dam of show-type puppies is, of course, the ideal selection; but these are usually difficult to obtain, no one being anxious to part with so valuable an asset. You just might strike it lucky, though, in which case you are off to a flying start. If you cannot find such a matron available, select a young bitch of finest background from top-producing lines who is herself of decent type, free of obvious faults, and of good quality.

Great attention should be paid to the pedigree of the bitch from whom you intend to breed. If not already known to you, try to see the sire and dam. It is generally agreed that someone starting with a breed should concentrate on a fine collection of topflight bitches and raise a few litters from these before considering keeping one's own stud dog. The practice of buying a stud and then breeding everything you own or acquire to that dog does not always work out well. It is better to take advantage of the many noted sires who are available to be used at stud, who represent all of the leading strains, and, in each case, to carefully select the one who in type and pedigree seems most compatible to each of your bitches, at least for your first several litters.

To summarize, if you want a "family dog" as a companion, it is best to buy it young and raise it according to the habits of your household. If you are buying a show dog, the more mature it is, the more certain you can be of its future beauty. If you are buying foundation stock for a kennel, then bitches are

and receive an identification of your dog, consisting of the name of the breed, the registered names and numbers of the sire and dam, the name of the breeder, and your dog's date of birth. If the litter of which your dog is a part is already recorded with the registry Club, then the litter number is sufficient

A four-week old litter of Pillow Talk babies owned by Lori and Tracy Kornfeld, Connecticut.

better, but they must be from the finest *producing* bloodlines.

When you buy a pure-bred dog that you are told is eligible for registration, you are entitled to receive from the seller an application form which will enable you to register your dog. If the seller cannot give you the application form, you should demand

identification.

Do not be misled by promises of papers at some later date. Demand a registration application form or proper identification as described above. If neither is supplied, do not buy the dog. Proper paper work is especially important in the purchase of show or breeding stock.

The Care of Your Bichon Puppy

The moment you decide to be the new owner of a puppy is not one second too soon to start planning for the puppy's arrival in your home. Both the new family member and you will find the transition period easier if your home is geared in advance of the arrival.

The first things to be prepared are a bed for the puppy and a place where you can pen him up for rest periods. Every dog should have a crate of its own from the very beginning, so that he will come to know and love it as his special place where he is safe and happy. It is an ideal arrangement, for when you want him to be free, the crate stays open. At other times you can securely latch it and know that the pup is safely out of mischief. If you travel with him, his crate comes along in the car; and, of course, in traveling by plane there is no alternative but to have a carrier for the dog. If you show your dog, you will want him upon occasion to be in a crate a good deal of the day. So from every consideration, a crate is a very sensible and sound investment in your puppy's future safety and happiness and for your own peace of mind.

The crates most desirable are the wooden ones with removable side panels, which are ideal for cold weather (with the panels in place to keep out drafts) and in hot weather (with the panels removed to allow better air circulation). Wire crates are all right in the summer, but they give no protection from cold or drafts. Aluminum crates, due to the manner in which the metal reflects surrounding temperatures, are not recommended. If it is cold, so is the metal of the crate; if it is hot, the crate becomes burning hot.

When you choose the puppy's crate, be certain that it is roomy enough not to become outgrown. The crate should have sufficient height so the dog can stand up in it as a mature dog and sufficient area so that he can stretch out full length when relaxed. When the puppy is young, first give him shredded newspaper as a bed; the papers can be replaced with a mat or turkish towels when the dog is older. Carpet remnants are great for the bottom of the crate, as they are inexpensive and in case of

Bichonhaven pups at play. Owned and bred by Angela Baldwin, Mansfield, Ontario.

accidents can be quite easily replaced. As the dog matures and is past the chewing age, a pillow or blanket in the crate is an appreciated comfort.

Sharing importance with the crate is a safe area in which the puppy can exercise and play. If you are an apartment dweller, a baby's playpen works out well for a young dog; for an older puppy use a portable exercise pen which you can use later when travelling with your dog or for dog shows. If you have a yard,

Cannondale Moete Chandon **in the boot. Bred by Miss. P. Page, Cattai, New South Wales, Australia.**

an area where he can be outside in safety should be fenced in prior to the dog's arrival at your home. This area does not need to be huge, but it does need to be made safe and secure. If you are in a suburban area where there are close neighbors, stockade fencing works out best, as then the neighbors are less aware of the dog and the dog cannot see and bark at everything passing by. If you are out in the country where no problems with neighbors are likely to occur, then regular chain-link fencing is fine. For added precaution in both cases, use a row of concrete blocks or railroad ties inside against the entire bottom of the fence; this precludes or at least considerably lessens the chances of your dog digging his way out.

Be advised that if yours is a single dog, it is very unlikely that it will get sufficient exercise just sitting in the fenced area, which is what most of them do when they are there alone. Two or more dogs will play and move themselves around, but one by itself does little more than make a leisurely tour once around the area to check things over and then lie down. You must include a daily walk or two in your plans if your puppy is to be rugged and well. Exercise is extremely important to a puppy's muscular development and to keep a mature dog fit and trim. So make sure that those exercise periods, or walks, a game of ball, and other such activities, are part of your daily program as a dog owner.

If your fenced area has an outside gate, provide a padlock and key and a strong fastening for it, and use them, so that the gate cannot be opened by others and the dog taken or turned free. The ultimate convenience in this regard is, of course, a door (unused for other purposes) from the house around which the fenced area can be enclosed, so that all you have to do is open the door and out into his area he goes. This arrangement is safest of all, as then you need not be using a gate, and it is easier in bad weather since then you can send the dog out without taking him and becoming soaked yourself at the same time. This is not always possible to manage, but if your house is arranged so that you could do it this way, you would never regret it due to the convenience and added safety thus provided. Fencing in the entire yard, with gates to be opened and closed whenever a

caller, deliveryman, postman, or some other person comes on your property, really is not safe at all because people not used to gates are frequently careless about closing and latching them *securely*. Many heartbreaking incidents have been brought about by someone carelessly half closing a gate (which the owner had thought to be firmly latched) and the dog wandering out. For greatest security a fenced *area* definitely takes precedence over a fenced *yard*.

The puppy will need a collar (one that fits now, not one to be grown into) and a lead from the moment you bring him home. Both should be an appropriate weight and type for his size. Also needed are a feeding dish and a water dish, both

A very sleepy *Maximillion* just can't keep his eyes open for the camera. One of the beautiful Bichons belonging to Toni and Michael Ambrosia, Belford, New Jersey.

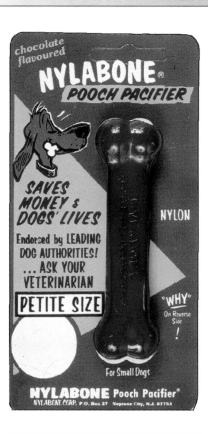

Select your Bichon's chewing devices with care. Nylabone® products such as the Puppybone®, Gumaknot®, and Nylaring®, are excellent safe and effective and are the best choices. Remember to buy the correct size for your Bichon.

made preferably of unbreakable material. Your pet supply shop should have an interesting assortment of these and other accessories from which you can choose. Then you will need grooming tools of the type the breeder recommends and some toys. Equally satisfactory is Nylabone®, a nylon bone that does not chip or splinter and that "frizzles" as the puppy chews, providing healthful gum massage. Avoid plastics and any sort of rubber toys, *particularly those with squeakers* which the puppy may remove and swallow. If you want a ball for the puppy to use when playing with him, select one of very hard construction made for this purpose and do not leave it alone with him because he may chew off and swallow bits of the rubber. Take the ball with you when the game is over. This also applies to some of those "tug of war" type rubber toys which are fun when used with the two of you for that purpose but again should *not* be left behind for the dog to work on with his teeth. Bits of swallowed rubber, squeakers, and other such foreign articles can wreak great havoc in the intestinal tract—do all you can to guard against them.

Ch. Kenningway's Heaven Forbid at age eight weeks leans on a plush friend from where she surveys the world with interest. Owned by Kendra James, Regina, Saskatchewan.

Too many changes all at once can be difficult for a puppy. For at least the first few days he is with you, keep him on the food and feeding schedule to which he is accustomed. Find out ahead of time from the breeder what he feeds his puppies, how frequently, and at what times of the day. Also find out what, if any, food supplements the breeder has been using and recommends. Then be prepared by getting in a supply of the same food so that you will have it there when you bring the puppy home. Once the puppy is accustomed to his new surroundings, then you can switch the type of food and schedule to fit your convenience, but for the first several days do it as the puppy expects.

Your selection of a veterinarian should also be attended to before the puppy comes home, because you should stop at the vet's office for the puppy to be checked

over as soon as you leave the breeder's premises. If the breeder is from your area, ask him for recommendations. Ask your dog-owning friends for their opinions of the local veterinarians, and see what their experiences with those available have been.

M. and A.'s Count D'Amour is all ready for the fun to start. Owned by Mr. and Mrs. Michael Ambrosio of Belford, New Jersey.

Choose someone whom several of your friends recommend highly, then contact him about your puppy, perhaps making an appointment to stop in at his office. If the premises are clean, modern, and well equipped, and if you like the veterinarian, make an appointment to bring the puppy in on the day of purchase. Be sure to obtain the puppy's health record from the breeder, including information on such things as shots and worming that the puppy has had.

JOINING THE FAMILY

Remember that, exciting and happy an occasion as it is for you, the puppy's move from his place of birth to your home can be, for him, a traumatic experience. His mother and littermates will be missed. He quite likely will be awed or frightened by the change of surroundings. The person on whom he depended will be gone. Everything should be planned to make his arrival at your home pleasant—to give him confidence and to help him realize that yours is a pretty nice place to be after all.

Never bring a puppy home on a holiday. There is just too much going on with people and gifts and excitement. If he is in honor of an "occasion," work it out so that his arrival will be a few days earlier, or perhaps even better, a few days later than the "occasion." Then your home will be back to its normal routine and the puppy can enjoy your undivided attention. Try not to bring the puppy home in the evening. Early morning is the ideal time, as then he has the opportunity of getting acquainted and the initial strangeness should wear off before bedtime. You will find it a more peaceful night that way. Allow the

puppy to investigate as he likes, under your watchful eye. If you already have a pet in the household, keep a careful watch that the relationship between the two gets off to a friendly start or you may quickly find yourself with a lasting problem. Much of the future attitude of each toward the other will depend on what takes place that first day, so keep your mind on what they are doing and let your other activities slide for the moment. Be careful not to let your older pet become jealous by paying more attention to the puppy than to him, as that will start a bad situation immediately.

If you have a child, here again it is important that the relationship start out well. Before the puppy is brought home, you should have a talk with the youngster. He must clearly understand that puppies are fragile and can easily be injured; therefore, they should not be teased, hurt, mauled, or overly rough-housed. A puppy is not an inanimate toy; it is a living thing with a right to be loved and handled respectfully, treatment which will reflect in the dog's attitude toward your child as both mature

This eight-week-old was a Singleton puppy who weighed two ounces at birth. His mother rejected him, necessitating his being entirely hand raised. Thanks to the love and dilligence of his human mother, Judith Beckman, this was successfully accomplished. Photo courtesy of Barbara Stubbs.

"I love you, too!" Mutual admiration obviously being exchanged between good friends! Photo courtesy of Gail Antetomaso, Massapequa, New York.

together. Never permit your children's playmates to mishandle the puppy, tormenting the puppy until it turns on the children in self-defense. Children often do not realize how rough is too rough. You, as a responsible adult, are obligated to assure that your puppy's relationship with children is a pleasant one.

Do not start out by spoiling your puppy. A puppy is usually pretty smart and can be quite demanding. What you had considered to be "just for tonight" may be accepted by the puppy as "for keeps." Be firm with him, strike a routine, and stick to it. The puppy will learn

more quickly this way, and everyone will be happier as a result. A radio playing softly or a dim night light are often comforting to a puppy as it gets accustomed to new surroundings and should be provided in preference to bringing the puppy to bed with you—unless, of course, you intend him to share the bed as a permanent arrangement.

SOCIALIZING AND TRAINING

Socialization and training of your puppy should start the very day of his arrival in your home. Never address him without calling him by name. A short, simple name is the easiest to teach as it catches the dog's attention quickly; avoid elaborate call names. Always address the dog by the same name, not a whole series of pet names; the latter will only confuse the puppy.

Use his name clearly, and call the puppy over to you when you see him awake and wandering about. When he comes, make a big fuss over him for being such a good dog. He thus will quickly associate the sound of his name with coming to you and a pleasant happening.

Several hours after the puppy's arrival is not too soon to start accustoming him to the feel of a light collar. He may hardly notice it; or he may struggle, roll over, and try to rub it off his neck with his paws. Divert his attention when this occurs by offering a tasty snack or a toy (starting a game with him) or by petting him. Before long he will have accepted the strange feeling around his neck and no longer appear aware of it. Next comes the lead. Attach it and then immediately take the puppy outside or otherwise try to divert his attention with things to see and sniff. He may struggle against the lead at first, biting at it and trying to free himself. Do not pull him with it at

this point; just hold the end loosely and try to follow him if he starts off in any direction. Normally his attention will soon turn to investigating his surroundings if he is outside or you have taken him into an unfamiliar room in your house; curiosity will take over and he will become interested in sniffing around the surroundings. Follow him with the lead slackly held until he seems to have completely forgotten about it; then try with gentle urging to get him to follow you. Don't be rough or jerk at him; just tug gently on the lead in short quick motions (steady pulling can become a battle of wills), repeating his name or trying to get him to follow

A three-week-old litter of future stars from Pillow Talk Bichons owned by Lori and Tracy Kornfeld, Ridgefield, Connecticut.

your hand which is holding a bite of food or an interesting toy. If you have an older lead-trained dog, then it should be a cinch to get the puppy to follow along after *him*. In any event the average puppy learns quite quickly and will soon be trotting along nicely on the lead. Once that point has been reached, the next step is to teach him to follow on your left side, or heel. This will not likely be accomplished all in one day; it should be done with short training periods over the course of several days until you are satisfied with the result.

During the course of house training your puppy, you will need to take him out frequently and at regular intervals: first thing in the morning directly from the crate, immediately after meals, after the puppy has been napping, or when you notice that the puppy is looking for a spot. Choose more or less the same place to take the puppy each time so that a pattern will be established. If he does not go immediately, do not return him to the house as he will probably relieve himself the moment he is inside. Stay out with him until he has finished; then be lavish with your praise for his good behavior. If you catch the puppy having an accident indoors, grab him firmly and rush him outside, sharply saying "No!" as you pick him up. If you do not see the accident occur, there is little point in doing anything except cleaning it up, as once it has happened and been forgotten, the puppy will most likely not even realize why you are scolding him.

Fun time! Two six-week-old Bichon puppies enjoying some play. Owned by Lori and Tracy Kornfeld, Ridgefield, Connecticut.

"Let's go Dad. Time for our spin" seems to be the thought of three-and-a-half-month-old Sammy. Irene B. and Joseph R. Libby owners, Enfield, Connecticut.

If you live in a big city or are away many hours at a time, having a dog that is trained to go on paper has some very definite advantages. To do this, one proceeds pretty much the same way as taking the puppy outdoors, except now you place the puppy on the newspaper at the proper time. The paper should always be kept in the same spot. An easy way to paper train a puppy if you have a playpen for it or an exercise pen is to line the area with newspapers; then gradually, every day or so, remove a section of newspaper until you are down to just one or two. The puppy acquires the habit of using the paper; and as the prepared area grows smaller, in the majority of cases the dog will continue to use whatever paper is still available. It is pleasant, if the dog is alone for an excessive length of time, to be able to feel that if he needs it the paper is there and will be used.

The puppy should form the habit of spending a certain amount of time in his crate, even when you are home. Sometimes the puppy will do this voluntarily, but if not, he should be taught to do so, which is accomplished by leading the puppy over by his collar, gently pushing him inside, and saying firmly, "Down" or "Stay." Whatever expression you use to give a command, stick to the very same one each time for each act.

At age ten-weeks, *Ch. Dove-Cote's Pillow Talk* shows off how a Bichon puppy of that age should look. By Ch. Dove Cote's Mr. Magoo, ROM ex Ch. Dove Cote's Pois-N-Ivory, ROM. Owned by Lori and Tracy Kornfeld, Ridgefield, Connecticut.

Repetition is the big thing in training—and so is association with what the dog is expected to do. When you mean "Sit," always say exactly that. "Stay" should mean *only* that the dog should remain where he receives the command. "Down" means something else again. Do not confuse the dog by shuffling the commands, as this will create training problems for you.

As soon as he has had his immunization shots, take your puppy with you whenever and wherever possible. There is nothing that will build a self-confident, stable dog like

socialization, and it is extremely important that you plan and give the time and energy necessary for this, whether your dog is to be a show dog or a pleasant, well-adjusted family member. Take your puppy in the car so that he will learn to enjoy riding and not become carsick, as dogs may do if they are infrequent travelers. Take him anywhere you are going where you are certain he will be welcome: visiting friends and relatives (if they do not have housepets who may resent the visit), busy shopping centers (keeping him always on lead), or just walking around the streets of your town. If someone admires him (as always seems to happen when one is out with puppies), encourage the stranger to pet and talk with him. Socialization of this type brings out the best in your puppy and helps him to grow up with a friendly outlook, liking the world and its inhabitants. The worst thing that can be done to a puppy's personality is to shelter him. By always keeping him at home away from things and people unfamiliar to him, you may be creating a personality problem for the mature dog that will be a cross for you to bear later on.

"Casper," alias Ch. Beau Cheval's Red Roses, one of the blooming beauties of the '90s, with handler David Roberts. Owners, David Ruml and Mrs. I. F. Zimmerman.

Breeding your Bichon Frise

The first responsibility of any person breeding dogs is to do so with care, forethought, and deliberation. It is inexcusable to breed more litters than you need to carry on your show program or to perpetuate your bloodlines. A responsible breeder should not cause a litter to be born (although doing so is not always feasible) the prospective owners of their puppies to see if they have suitable facilities for keeping a dog, to find out if they understand the responsibility involved, and to make certain if all members of the household are in accord regarding the desirability of owning one.

Am. Can. Ch. Tondia's Bright Eyes-Bushy Tail proudly surveys his puppies. Norma J. Dirszowsky, owner Udora, Ontario.

without definite plans for the safe and happy disposition of the puppies.

A responsible dog breeder makes absolutely certain, so far as is humanly possible, that the home to which one of his puppies will go is a good home, one that offers proper care and an enthusiastic owner. To be admired are those breeders who insist on visiting

All breeders should carefully check out the credentials of prospective purchasers to be sure that the puppy is being placed in responsible hands.

No breeder ever wants a puppy or grown dog he has raised to wind up in an animal shelter, in an experimental laboratory, or as a victim of a speeding car. While complete control of such a situation may be

Gail Antetomaso with her well-known *Ch. Mr. Magic*, and one of his daughters.

impossible, it is important to make every effort to turn over dogs to responsible people. When selling a puppy, it is a good idea to do so with the understanding that should it become necessary to place the dog in other hands, the purchaser will first contact you, the breeder. You may want to help in some way, possibly by buying or taking back the dog or placing it elsewhere. It is not fair to sell puppies and then never again give a thought to

Like father, like daughter. *Ch. Gayla's Mr. Magic of Glenelfred* with daughter. Gail Antetomasa, owner.

their welfare. Family problems arise, people may be forced to move where dogs are prohibited, or people just grow bored with a dog and its care. Thus the dog becomes a victim. You, as the dog's breeder, should concern yourself with the welfare of each of your dogs and see to it that the dog remains in good hands.

The final obligation every dog owner shares, be there just one dog or an entire kennel involved, is that of making detailed, explicit plans for the future of these dearly loved animals in the event of the owner's death. Far too many people are apt to procrastinate and leave this very important matter unattended to, feeling that everything will work out or that "someone will see to

them." Neither is too likely, at least not to the benefit of the dogs, unless you have done some advance planning which will assure their future well-being.

Life is filled with the unexpected, and even the youngest, healthiest, most robust of us may be the victim of a fatal accident or sudden illness. The fate of your dogs, so entirely in your hands, should never be left to chance. If you have not already done so, please get together with your lawyer and set up a clause in your will specifying what you want done with each of your dogs, to whom they will be entrusted (after first making absolutely certain that the person selected is willing and able to assume the responsibility), and telling the locations of all registration papers, pedigrees, and kennel records. Just think of the possibilities which might happen otherwise! If there is another family member who shares your love of the dogs, that is good and you have less to worry about. But if your heirs are not dog-oriented, they will hardly know how to proceed or how to cope with the dogs themselves, and they may wind up disposing of or caring for your dogs in a manner that would break your heart were you around to know about it.

It is advisable to have in your will specific instructions concerning each of your dogs. A friend, also a dog person who regards his or her own dogs with the same concern and esteem as you do, may agree to take over their care until they can be placed accordingly and will make certain that all will work out as you have planned. This person's name and phone number can be prominently displayed in your van or car and in your wallet. Your lawyer can be made aware of this fact. This can be spelled out in your will. The friend can have a signed check of yours to be used in case of an emergency or accident when you are traveling with

the dogs; this check can be used to cover his or her expense to come and take over the care of your dogs should anything happen to make it impossible for you to do so. This is the least any dog owner should do in preparation for the time their dogs suddenly find themselves alone. There have been so many sad cases of dogs unprovided for by their loving owners, left to heirs who couldn't care less and who disposed of them in any way at all to get rid of them, or left to heirs who kept and neglected them under the misguided idea that they were providing them "a fine home with lots of freedom." These misfortunes must be

Puppies and one very proud mom, *Ch. Dove Cote's Cracker Jack*, at play. Owned by Lori and Tracy Kornfeld, Ridgefield, Connecticut.

prevented from befalling your own dogs who have meant so much to you!

Conscientious breeders feel quite strongly that the only possible reason for producing puppies is the ambition to improve and uphold quality and temperament within the breed—definitely *not* because one hopes to make a quick cash profit on a mediocre litter, which never seems to work out that way in the long run and which accomplishes little beyond perhaps adding to the nation's heartbreaking number of unwanted canines. The only reason ever for breeding a litter is, with conscientious people, a desire to improve the quality of dogs in their own kennel or, as pet owners, to add to the number of dogs they themselves own with a puppy or two from their present favorites. In either case, breeding should not take place unless one definitely has prospective owners for as many puppies as the litter may contain, lest you find yourself with several fast-growing young dogs and no homes in which to place them.

THE BROOD BITCH

Bitches should not be mated earlier than their second season, by which time they should be from fifteen to eighteen months old. Many breeders prefer to wait and finish the championships of their show bitches before breeding them, as pregnancy can be a disaster to a show coat and getting the bitch back in shape again takes time. When you have decided what will be the proper time, start watching at least several months ahead

A family in which to take pride, as indeed seems to be the case with *Ch. Kenningway's Charisma* as she sits among her litter of eight gorgeous babies by *Ch. Kenningway's Mercedes Benz.* All are owned by Kendra James, Regina, Saskatchewan.

for what you feel would be the perfect mate to best complement your bitch's quality and bloodlines. Subscribe to the magazines which feature your breed exclusively and to some which cover all breeds in order to familiarize yourself with outstanding stud dogs in areas other than your own, for there is no necessity nowadays to limit your choice to a local dog unless you truly like him and feel that he is the most suitable. It is quite usual to ship a bitch to a stud dog a distance away, and this generally works out with no ill effects. The important thing is that you need a stud dog strong in those features where your bitch is weak, a dog whose bloodlines are compatible with hers. Compare the

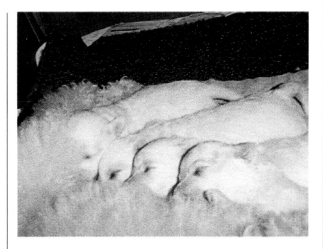

background of both your bitch and the stud dog under consideration, paying particular attention to the quality of the puppies from bitches with backgrounds similar to your bitch's. If the puppies have been of the type and quality you admire, then this dog would seem a sensible choice for yours, too.

Two-week-old Bichon Frise babies "at the dinner table" alongside their mother. Owned by Ed and Anne Jones, Virginia.

Such a pair of Charmers! *Ch. Prince Rudolph* and his mother *Ch. Heidi* enjoying a beautiful day at the home of their owners Irene and Joseph Libby in Enfield, Connecticut.

Dove Cote's Crackerjack with four-day-old puppies. Lori and Tracy Kornfeld, owners, Ridgefield, Connecticut.

Stud fees may be a few hundred dollars, sometimes even more under special situations for a particularly successful sire. It is money well spent, however. *Do not* ever breed to a dog because he is less expensive than the others unless you honestly believe that he can sire the kind of puppies who will be a credit to your kennel and your breed.

Contacting the owners of the stud dogs you find interesting will bring you pedigrees and pictures which you can then study in relation to your bitch's pedigree and conformation. Discuss your plans with other breeders who are knowledgeable (including the one who bred your own bitch). You may not always receive an entirely unbiased opinion (particularly if the person

giving it also has an available stud dog), but one learns by discussion so listen to what they say, consider their opinions, and then you may be better qualified to form your own opinion.

As soon as you have made a choice, phone the owner of the stud dog you wish to use to find out if this will be agreeable. You will be asked about the bitch's health, soundness, temperament, and freedom from serious faults. A copy of her pedigree may be requested, as might a picture of her. A discussion of her background over the telephone may be sufficient to assure the stud's owner that she is suitable for the stud dog and that she is of type, breeding, and quality herself, capable of producing the kind of puppies for which the stud is noted. The owner of a top-quality stud is often extremely selective in the bitches permitted to be bred to his dog, in an effort to keep the standard of his puppies high. The owner of a stud dog may require that the bitch be tested for brucellosis, which should be attended to not more than a month previous to the breeding.

Check out which airport will be most convenient for the person meeting and returning the bitch, if she is to be shipped, and also what airlines use that airport. You will find that the airlines are also apt to have special requirements concerning acceptance of animals for shipping. These include weather limitations and types of crates which are acceptable. The weather limits have to do with extreme heat and extreme cold at the point of destination, as some airlines will not fly dogs into temperatures above or below certain levels, fearing for their safety. The crate problem is a simple one, since, if your own crate is not suitable, most of the airlines have specially designed crates available for purchase at a fair and moderate price. It is a good plan to purchase one of these if you intend to be shipping dogs with any sort of frequency. They are made of fiberglass and are the safest type to use for shipping.

Normally you must notify the airline several days in advance to make a reservation, as they are able to accommodate only a certain number of dogs on each flight. Plan on shipping the bitch on about her eighth or ninth day of season, but be careful to avoid shipping her on a weekend when schedules often vary and freight offices are apt to be closed. Whenever you can, ship your bitch on a direct flight. Changing planes always carries a certain amount of risk of a dog being overlooked or

Can. Ch. Kenningway Pennies From Heaven owned by Kendra James and Regina, Saskatchewan. "Penny" produced five champions including Ch. Kenningway's Seventh Heaven, at Snopuff Kennels, who produced three litters, including two BIS dogs and a National Specialty winner.

wrongly routed at the middle stop, so avoid this danger if at all possible. The bitch must be accompanied by a health certificate which you must obtain from your veterinarian before taking her to the airport. Usually it will be necessary to have the bitch at the airport about two hours prior to flight time. Before finalizing arrangements, find out from the stud's owner at what time of day it will be most convenient to have the bitch picked up promptly upon arrival.

It is simpler if you can bring the bitch to the stud dog yourself. Some people feel that the trauma of the flight may cause the bitch to not conceive; and, of course, undeniably there is a slight risk in shipping which can be avoided if you are able to drive the bitch to her destination. Be sure to leave yourself sufficient time to assure your arrival at the right time for her for breeding (normally the tenth to fourteenth day following the first signs of color); and remember that if you want the bitch bred twice, you should allow a day to elapse between the two matings. Do not expect the stud's owner to house you while you are there. Locate a nearby motel that takes dogs and make that your headquarters.

Just prior to the time your bitch is due in season, you should take her to visit your veterinarian. She should be checked for worms and should receive all the booster shots for which she is due plus one for parvovirus, unless she has had the latter shot fairly recently. The brucellosis test can also be done then, and the health certificate can be obtained for shipping if she is to travel by air. Should the bitch be at all overweight, now is the time to get the surplus off. She should be in good condition, neither underweight nor overweight, at the time of breeding.

The moment you notice the swelling of the vulva, for which you should be checking daily as the time for her season approaches, and the appearance of color, immediately contact the stud's owner and settle on the day for shipping or make the appointment for your arrival with the bitch for breeding. If you are shipping the bitch, the stud fee check should be mailed immediately, leaving ample time for it to have been received when the bitch arrives and the mating takes place. Be sure to call the airline, making her reservation at that time, too.

Do not feed the bitch within a few hours before shipping her. Be certain that she has had a drink of water and been well exercised before closing her in the crate. Several layers of newspapers, topped with some shredded newspaper, make a good bed and can be discarded when she arrives at her destination; these can be replaced with fresh newspapers for her return home. Remember that the bitch should be brought to the airport about two hours before flight time, as sometimes the airlines refuse to accept late arrivals.

If you are taking your bitch by car, be certain that you will arrive at a reasonable time of day. Do not appear late in the evening. If your arrival in town is not until late, get a good night's sleep at your motel and contact the stud's owner first thing in the morning. If possible, leave children and relatives at home, as they will only be in the way and perhaps unwelcome by the stud's owner. Most stud dog owners prefer not to have any unnecessary people on hand during the actual mating.

After the breeding has taken place, if you wish to sit and visit for awhile and the stud's owner has the time, return the bitch to her crate in your car (first ascertaining, of course, that the temperature is comfortable for her and that there is proper ventilation). She should not be permitted to urinate for at least one hour following the breeding. This is the time when you attend to the business part of the transaction. Pay the stud fee, upon which you should receive your breeding certificate and, if you do not already have it, a copy of the stud dog's pedigree. The owner of the stud dog does not sign or furnish a litter registration application until the puppies have been born.

Upon your return home, you can settle down and plan in happy anticipation a wonderful litter of puppies. A word of caution! Remember that although she has been bred, your bitch is still an interesting target for all male dogs, so guard her carefully for the

Ch. Windstar Fig Newton, sired by Ch. Glen Elfred's Mr. Chips ex Ch. Belinda de Windstar. Owned by Estelle Kellerman. This typey and high quality bitch has produced multiple Group winners. She is handled by Mrs. Kellerman's daughter Wendy.

next week or until you are absolutely certain that her season has entirely ended. This would be no time to have any unfortunate incident with another dog.

THE STUD DOG

Choosing the best stud dog to complement your bitch is often very difficult. The two principal factors to be considered should be the stud's conformation and his pedigree. Conformation is fairly obvious; you want a dog that is typical of the breed in the words of the Standard of perfection. Understanding pedigrees is a bit more subtle since the pedigree lists the ancestry of the dog and involves individuals and bloodlines with which you may not be entirely familiar.

Aust., Fr., Ger., Sws., Int. Ch. Looping De La Buthiere sired by Int. Ch. If De La Buthiere ex Int. Ch. Vania de Villa Sainval. Looping is the only International Champion to come to Australia and be shown. Owned by Azara Kennels, F.C. Valley and R.W. Van Voorst, Ivanhoe, Victoria.

To a novice in the breed, the correct interpretation of a pedigree may at first be difficult to grasp. Study the pictures and text of this book and you will find many names of important bloodlines and members of the breed. Also make an effort to discuss the various dogs behind the proposed stud with some of the more experienced breeders, starting with the breeder of your own bitch. Frequently these folks will be familiar with many of the dogs in question, will be able to offer opinions of them, and may have access to additional pictures which you would benefit by seeing. It is very important that the stud's pedigree be harmonious with that of the bitch you plan on breeding to him. Do not rush out and breed to the latest winner with no thought of whether or not he can produce true quality. By no means are all great show dogs great producers. It is the producing record of the dog in question, and the dogs and bitches from which he has come, that should be the basis on which you make your choice.

Breeding dogs is never a money-making operation. By the time you pay a stud fee, care for the bitch during pregnancy, whelp the litter, and rear the puppies through their early shots, worming, and so on, you will be fortunate to break even financially once the puppies have been sold. Your chances of doing this are greater if you are breeding for a show-quality litter which will bring you higher prices, as the pups are sold as show prospects. Therefore, your wisest investment is to use the best dog available for your bitch regardless of the cost; then you should wind up with more valuable puppies. Remember that it is equally costly to raise mediocre puppies as it is top ones, and your chances of financial return are better on the latter. Breeding to the most excellent, most suitable stud dog you can find is the only sensible thing to do, and it is poor economy to quibble over the amount you are paying in a stud fee.

It will be your decision as to which course you follow when you breed your bitch, as there are three options: linebreeding, inbreeding, and outcrossing. Each of these methods has its supporters and its detractors! Linebreeding is breeding a bitch to a dog belonging originally to the same canine family, being descended from the same ancestors, such as half-brother to half-sister,

grandsire to granddaughter, niece to uncle (and vice-versa) or cousin to cousin. Inbreeding is breeding father to daughter, mother to son, or full-brother to sister. Outcross breeding is breeding a dog and a bitch with no or only a few mutual ancestors.

Linebreeding is probably the safest course, and the one most likely to bring results, for the novice breeder. The more sophisticated inbreeding should be left to the experienced, longtime breeders who throroughly

Helen and Gus Temmel of Dunedin, Florida, photographed here during the early 1970s with their famous winning Bichon *Ch. Roger Bontemps de la Stonehedge, CDX*, son of Ch. Chaminade Syncopation, and a Norwich Terrier.

Bobander Theme For A Dream at Spelga, and *Bobander Love In The Air For Spelga*. Owned by Pat and Glen Keery, Spelga Kennels, Hillsborough, County Down, Ireland.

know and understand the risks and the possibilities involved with a particular line. It is usually done in an effort to intensify some ideal feature in that strain. Outcrossing is the reverse of inbreeding, an effort to introduce improvement in a specific feature needing correction, such as a shorter back, better movement, more correct head or coat, and so on.

It is the serious breeder's ambition to develop a strain or bloodline of their own, one strong in qualities for which their dogs will become distinguished. However, it must be realized that this will

involve time, patience, and at least several generations before the achievement can be claimed. The safest way to embark on this plan, as previously mentioned, is by the selection and breeding of one or two bitches, the best you can buy and from top-producing kennels. In the beginning you do *not* really have to own a stud dog. In the long run it is less expensive and sounder judgement to pay a stud fee when you are ready to breed a bitch than to purchase a stud dog and feed him all year; a stud dog does not win any popularity contests with owners of bitches to be bred until he becomes a champion, has been successfully Specialed for a while, and has been at least moderately advertised, all of which adds up to quite a healthy expenditure.

The wisest course for the inexperienced breeder just starting out in dogs is to keep the best bitch puppy from the first several litters. After that you may wish to consider keeping your own stud dog, if there has been a particularly handsome male in one of your litters that you feel has great potential or if you know where there is one available that you are interested in, with the feeling that he would work in nicely with the breeding program on which you have embarked. By this time, with several litters already born, your eye should have developed to a point enabling you to make a wise choice, either from one of your own litters or from among dogs you have seen that appear suitable.

The greatest care should be taken in the selection of your own stud dog. He must be of true type and highest quality as he may be responsible for siring many puppies each year, and he should come from a line of excellent dogs on both sides of his pedigree which themselves are, and which are descended from, successful producers. This dog should have no glaring faults in conformation; he should be of such quality that he can hold his own in keenest competition within his breed. He should be in good health, be virile and be a keen stud dog, a proven sire able to transmit his correct qualities to his puppies. Need one say that such a dog will be enormously expensive

Aust. Ch. Rock Court Snow Queen is the dam; *Aust. Ch. Tejada Venusbay Rider*, sire; *Aust. Ch. Shabrand Snow Rider*, son; and *Aust. Ch. Shabrand Snow White*, daughter. All owned by Miss P.Page, Cattai, New South Wales.

unless you have the good fortune to produce him in one of your own litters? To buy and use a lesser stud dog, however, is downgrading your breeding program unnecessarily since there are so many dogs fitting the description of a fine stud whose services can be used on payment of a stud fee.

You should never breed to an unsound dog or one with any serious disqualifying faults according to the breed's standard. Not all champions by any means pass along their best features; and by the same token, occasionally you will find a great one who can pass along his best features but never gained his championship title due to some unusual

Ch. Dove-Cote's Valentine Heidi with an adorable Bichon puppy. Owned by Joseph Libby, Enfield, Connecticut.

circumstances. The information you need about a stud dog is what type of puppies he has produced, and with what bloodlines, and whether or not he possesses the bloodlines and attributes considered characteristic of the best in your breed.

If you go out to buy a stud dog, obviously he will not be a puppy, but rather a fully mature and proven male with as many of the best attributes as possible. True, he will be an expensive investment, but if you choose and make his selection with care and forethought, he may well prove to be one of the best investments you have ever made.

Of course, the most exciting of all is when a young male you have decided to keep from one of your litters, due to his tremendous show potential, turns out to be a stud dog such as we have described. In this case he should be managed with care, for he is a valuable property that can contribute inestimably to this breed as a whole and to your own kennel specifically.

Do not permit your stud dog to be used until he is about a year old, and even then he should be bred to a mature, proven matron accustomed to breeding who will make his first

Two lovely lady Bichons, litter sisters of the 1970s-1980s period who lived to be close to 17 years old. They were sired by Paw Paw Ulysses ex Lilbit Chez Rivage d'Ami. The sisters were bred by Dolores Benefiel and owned by Eleanor Grassick.

experience pleasant and easy. A young dog can be put off forever by a maiden bitch who fights and resists his advances. Never allow this to happen. Always start a stud dog out with a bitch who is mature, has been bred previously, and is of even temperament. The first breeding should be performed in quiet surroundings with only you and one other person to hold the bitch. Do not make it a circus, as the experience will determine the dog's outlook about future stud work. If he does not enjoy the first experience or associates it with any unpleasantness, you may well have a problem in the future.

Your young stud must permit help with the breeding, as later there will be bitches who will not be cooperative. If right from the beginning you are there helping him and praising him, whether or not your assistance is actually needed, he will expect and accept this as a matter of course when a difficult bitch comes along.

Things to have handy before introducing your dog and the bitch are K-Y jelly (the only lubricant which should be used) and a length of gauze with which to muzzle the bitch should it be necessary to keep her from biting you or the dog. Some bitches put up a fight; others are calm. It is best to be prepared.

At the time of the breeding, the stud fee comes due, and it is expected that it will be paid promptly. Normally a return service is offered in case the bitch misses or fails to produce one live puppy. Conditions of the service are what the stud dog's owner makes them, and there are no standard rules covering this. The stud fee is paid for the act, not the result. If the bitch fails to conceive, it is customary for the owner to offer a free return service; but this is a courtesy and not to be considered a right, particularly in the case of a proven stud who is siring consistently and whose fault the failure obviously is *not*. Stud dog owners are always anxious to see their clients get good value and to have, in the ring, winning young stock by their dog; therefore, very few refuse to mate the second time. It is wise, however, for both parties to have the terms of the transaction clearly understood at the time of the breeding.

If the return service has been provided and the bitch has missed a second time, that is considered to be the end of the matter and the owner would be expected to pay a further fee if it is felt that the bitch should be given a third chance with the stud dog. The management of a stud dog and his visiting bitches is quite a task, and a stud fee has usually been well earned when one service has been achieved, let alone by repeated visits from the same bitch.

The accepted litter is one live puppy. It is wise to have printed a breeding certificate which the owner of the stud dog and the owner of the bitch both sign. This should list in detail the conditions of the breeding as well as the dates of the mating.

Upon occasion, arrangements other than a stud fee in cash are made for a breeding, such as the owner of the stud taking a pick-of-the-litter puppy in lieu of money. This should be clearly specified on the breeding certificate along with the terms of the age at which the stud's owner will select the puppy, whether it is to be a specific sex, or whether it is to be the pick of the entire litter.

The price of a stud fee varies according to circumstances. Usually, to prove a young stud dog, his owner will allow the first breeding to be quite inexpensive. Then, once a bitch has become pregnant by him, he becomes a "proven stud" and the fee rises accordingly for bitches that follow. The sire of championship quality puppies will bring a stud fee of at least the purchase price of one show puppy as the accepted "rule-of-thumb." Until at least one champion by your stud dog has finished, the fee will remain equal to the price of one pet puppy. When his list of champions starts to grow, so does the amount of the stud fee. For a top-producing sire of champions, the stud fee will rise accordingly.

Almost invariably it is the bitch who comes to the stud dog for the breeding. Immediately upon having selected the stud dog you wish to use, discuss the possibility with the owner of that dog. It is the stud dog owner's prerogative to refuse to breed any bitch deemed unsuitable for this dog. Stud fee and method of payment should be stated at this time and a decision reached on whether it is to be a full cash transaction at the time of the mating or a pick-of-the-litter puppy, usually at eight weeks of age.

If the owner of the stud dog must travel to an airport to meet the bitch and ship her for the flight home, an additional charge will be made for time, tolls, and gasoline based on the stud owner's proximity to the airport. The stud fee includes board for the day on the bitch's arrival through two days for breeding, with a day in between. If it is necessary that the bitch remain longer, it is very likely that additional board will be charged at the normal per-day rate for the breed.

Be sure to advise the stud's owner as soon as you know that your bitch is in season so that the stud dog will be available. This is especially important because if he is a dog being shown, he and his owner may be unavailable, owing to the dog's absence from home.

As the owner of a stud dog being offered to the public, it is essential that you have proper facilities for the care of visiting bitches. Nothing can be worse than a bitch being insecurely housed and slipping out to become lost or bred by the wrong dog. If you are taking people's valued bitches into your kennel or home, it is imperative that you provide them with comfortable, secure housing and good care while they are your responsibility.

There is no dog more valuable than the proven sire of champions, Group winners, and Best in Show dogs. Once you have such an animal, guard his reputation well and do *not* permit him to be bred to just any bitch that comes along. It takes two to make the puppies; even the most dominant stud cannot do it all himself, so never permit him to breed a bitch you consider unworthy. Remember that when the puppies arrive, it will be your stud dog who will be blamed for any lack of quality, while the bitch's shortcomings will be quickly and conveniently overlooked.

Going into the actual management of the mating is a bit superfluous here. If you have had previous experience in breeding a dog and bitch, you will know how the mating is done. If you do not have such experience, you should not attempt to follow directions given in a book but should have a veterinarian, breeder friend, or handler there to help you with the first few times. You do not turn the dog and bitch loose together and await developments, as too many things can go wrong and you may altogether miss getting the bitch bred. Someone should hold the dog and the bitch (one person each) until the "tie" is made and these two people should stay with them during the entire act.

If you get a complete tie, probably only the one mating is absolutely necessary. However, especially with a maiden bitch or one that has come a long distance for this breeding, a follow-up with a second breeding is preferred, leaving one day in between the two matings. In this way there will be little or no chance of the bitch missing.

Once the tie has been completed and the dogs release, be certain that the male's penis goes completely back within its sheath. He should be allowed a drink of water and a short walk, and then he should be put into his crate or somewhere alone where he can settle down. Do not allow him to be with other dogs for a while as they will notice the odor of the bitch on him, and,

Ch. Chismene Man About Town from Australia. A multiple Group One placement winner belonging to Mrs. J. Jeffrey of Sydney, Australia.

particularly with other males present, he may become involved in a fight.

PREGNANCY, WHELPING, AND THE LITTER

Once the bitch has been bred and is back at home, remember to keep an ever watchful eye that no other males get to her until at least the twenty-second day of her season has passed. Until then, it will still be possible for an unwanted breeding to take place, which at this point would be catastrophic. Remember that she actually can have two separate litters by two different dogs, so take care.

In other ways, she should be treated normally. Controlled exercise is good and necessary for the bitch throughout her pregnancy, tapering it off to just several short walks daily, preferably on lead, as she reaches her seventh week. As her time grows close, be careful about her jumping or playing too roughly.

The theory that a bitch should be overstuffed with food when pregnant is a poor one. A fat bitch is never an easy whelper, so the overfeeding you consider good for her may well turn out to be a hindrance later on. During the first few weeks of pregnancy, your bitch should be fed her normal diet. At four to five weeks

Enjoue My Buddy owned by Ed and Anne Jones. Especially significant on this dog are the perfect Bichon head, expression, and temperament.

along, calcium should be added to her food. At seven weeks her food may be increased if she seems to crave more than she is getting, and a meal of canned milk (mixed with an equal amount of water) should be introduced. If she is fed just once a day, add another meal rather than overload her with too much at one time. If twice a day is her schedule, then a bit more food can be added to each feeding.

A week before the pups are due, your bitch should be introduced to her whelping box so that she will be accustomed to it and feel at home there when the puppies arrive. She should be encouraged to sleep there but permitted to come and go as she wishes. The box should be roomy enough for her to lie down and stretch out in but not too large, lest the pups have more room than is needed in which to roam and possibly get chilled by going too far away from their mother. Be sure that the box has a "pig rail"; this will prevent the puppies from being crushed against the sides. The room in which the box is placed, either in your home or in the kennel, should be kept at about 70 degrees Fahrenheit. In winter it may be necessary to have an infrared lamp over the whelping box, in which case be careful not to place it too low or close to the puppies.

Newspapers will become a very important commodity, so start collecting them well in advance to have a big pile handy for the whelping box. With a litter of puppies, one never seems to have papers enough, so the higher pile to start with, the better off you will be. Other necessities for whelping time are clean, soft turkish towels, scissors, and a bottle of alcohol.

You will know that her time is very near when your bitch becomes restless, wandering in and out of her box and out of the room. She may refuse food, and at that point her temperature will start to drop. She will dig at and tear up the newspapers in her box, shiver, and generally look uncomfortable. Only you should be with your bitch at this time. She does not need spectators; and several people hanging over her, even though they may be family members whom she knows, may upset her to the point where she may harm the puppies. You should remain nearby, quietly watching, not fussing or hovering; speak calmly and frequently to her to instill confidence. Eventually she will settle down in her box and begin panting; contractions will follow. Soon thereafter a puppy will start to emerge, sliding out with the contractions. The mother immediately should open the sac, sever the cord with her teeth, and then clean up the puppy. She will also eat the placenta, which you should permit. Once the puppy is cleaned, it should be placed next to the bitch unless she is showing signs of having the next one immediately. Almost at once the puppy will start looking for a nipple on which to nurse, and you should ascertain that it is able to latch on successfully.

If the puppy is a breech (*i.e.*, born feet first), you must watch carefully for it to be completely delivered as quickly as possible and for the sac to be removed quickly so that the puppy does not drown. Sometimes even a normally positioned birth will seem extremely slow in coming. Should this occur, you might take a clean towel, and as the bitch contracts, pull the puppy out, doing so gently and with utmost care. If, once the puppy is delivered, it shows little signs of life, take a rough turkish towel and massage the puppy's chest by rubbing quite briskly back and forth. Continue this for about fifteen minutes, and be sure that the mouth is free of liquid. It may be necessary to try mouth-to-mouth breathing, which is begun by pressing the puppy's jaws open and, using a finger, depressing the tongue which may be stuck to the roof of the mouth. Then place your mouth against the puppy's and blow hard down the puppy's throat. Rub the puppy's chest with the towel again and try artificial respiration, pressing the sides of the chest together slowly and rhythmically—in and out,

in and out. Keep trying one method or the other for at least twenty minutes before giving up. You may be rewarded with a live puppy who otherwise would not have made it.

If you are successful in bringing the puppy around, do not immediately put it back with the mother as it should be kept extra warm. Put it in a cardboard box on an electric heating pad or, if it is the time of year when your heat is running, near a radiator or near the fireplace or stove. As soon as the rest of the litter has been born, it then can join the others.

An hour or more may elapse between puppies, which is fine so long as the bitch seems comfortable and is neither straining nor

This pretty Bichon lady is *Ch. L'Harve Joyeuox Enjoue Spirit* owned by Ed and Anne Jones, Charles City, Virginia. Note the georgous head, eyes and expression of this outstanding bitch, which, along with her personality and disposition, represent Bichon character at it's finest.

contracting. She should not be permitted to remain unassisted for more than an hour if she does continue to contract. This is when you should get her to your veterinarian, whom you should already have alerted to the possibility of a problem existing. He should examine her and perhaps give her a shot of Pituitrin. In some cases the veterinarian may find that a Caesarean section is necessary due to a puppy being lodged in a manner making normal delivery impossible. Sometimes this is caused by an abnormally large puppy, or it may just be that the puppy is simply turned in the wrong position. If the bitch does require a Caesarean section, the puppies already born must be kept warm in their cardboard box with a heating pad under the box.

Once the section is done, get the bitch and the puppies home. Do not attempt to put the puppies in with the bitch until she has regained consciousness, as she may unknowingly hurt them. But do get them back to her as soon as possible for them to start nursing.

Should the mother lack milk at this time, the puppies must be fed by hand, kept very warm, and held onto the mother's teats several times a day in order to stimulate and encourage the secretion of milk, which should start shortly.

Assuming that there has been no problem and that the bitch has whelped naturally, you should insist that she go out to exercise, staying just long enough to make herself comfortable. She can be offered a bowl of milk and a biscuit, but then she should settle down with her family. Freshen the whelping box for her with newspapers while she is taking this respite so that she and the puppies will have a clean bed.

Unless some problem arises, there is little you must do for the puppies until they become three to four weeks old. Keep the box clean and supplied with fresh newspapers the first few days, but then turkish towels should be tacked down to the bottom of the box so that the puppies will have traction as they move about.

If the bitch has difficulties with her milk supply, or if you should be so unfortunate as to lose her, then you must be prepared to either hand-feed or tube-feed the puppies if they are to survive. Tube-feeding is so much faster and easier. If the bitch is available, it is best that she continues to clean and care for the puppies in the normal manner, excepting for the food supplements you will provide. If it is impossible for her to do this, then after every feeding you must

Have your veterinarian teach you how to tube-feed. You will find that it is really quite simple.

After a normal whelping, the bitch will require additional food to enable her to produce sufficient

gently rub each puppy's abdomen with wet cotton to make it urinate, and the rectum should be gently rubbed to open the bowels.

Newborn puppies must be fed every three to four hours around the clock. The puppies must be kept warm during this time.

milk. In addition to being fed twice daily, she should be given some canned milk several times each day.

When the puppies are two weeks old, their nails should be clipped, as they are needle sharp at this age and can hurt or damage the mother's teats and

Ch. Dove-Cote's Valentine Heidi **owned by Joseph Libby of Enfield, Connecticut. A noted winner and producer.**

stomach as the pups hold on to nurse.

Between three and four weeks of age, the puppies should begin to be weaned. Scraped beef (prepared by scraping it off slices of beef with a spoon so that none of the gristle is included) may be offered in very small quantities a couple of times daily for the first few days. Then by the third day you can mix puppy chow with warm water as directed on the package, offering it four times daily. By now the mother should be kept away from the puppies and out of the box for several hours at a time so that when they have reached five weeks of age she is left in with them only overnight. By the time the puppies are six weeks old, they should be entirely weaned and receiving only occasional visits from their mother.

Most veterinarians recommend a temporary DHL (distemper, hepatitis, leptospirosis) shot when the puppies are six weeks of age. This remains effective for about two weeks. Then at eight weeks of age, the puppies should receive the series of permanent shots for DHL protection. It is also a good idea to discuss with your vet the advisability of having your puppies inoculated against the dreaded parvovirus at the same time. Each time the pups go to the vet for shots, you should bring stool samples so that they can be examined for worms. Worms go through various stages of development and may be present in a stool sample even though the sample does not test positive in every checkup. So do not neglect to keep careful watch on this.

The puppies should be fed four times daily until they are three months old. Then you can cut back to three feedings daily. By the time the puppies are six months of age, two meals daily are sufficient. Some people feed their dogs twice daily throughout their lifetime; others go to one meal daily when the puppy becomes one year of age.

The ideal age for puppies to go to their new homes is between eight and twelve weeks, although some puppies successfully adjust to a new home when they are six weeks old. Be sure that they go to their new owners accompanied by a description of the diet you've been feeding them and a schedule of the shots they have already received and those they still need. These should be included with the registration application and a copy of the pedigree.

Ch. Gaylon's Mr. Magic of Glenelfred Owned by Gail Antetomaso of Massapequa, New York.

Your Well-Groomed Bichon

by Cliff Steele

The art of turning out a beautifully groomed Bichon is one requiring not just the desire to do so but the talent, artistic eye, and expertise. Many people realize how the dog *should* look but find it extremely difficult if not impossible to bring this happy culmination of their efforts about. Meanwhile others do so with ease and assurance, seeming to know almost instinctively exactly what will be the most becoming to any dog upon which they work.

Respecting as I do the importance of coat care, grooming, and scissoring to a winning Bichon Frise,

some very special thought went into the selection of someone to oversee, make suggestions, and demonstrate how it should be done for this section of our new Bichon book. On many occasions I have noted the well-turned-out picture presented by the highly successful professional handler and Bichon expert Clifford Steel. Thus it was to him that I went in hopes that he might have the time and interest to take over this task. He agreed, to my delight, and so we most proudly bring you his demonstration of grooming a Bichon along with other

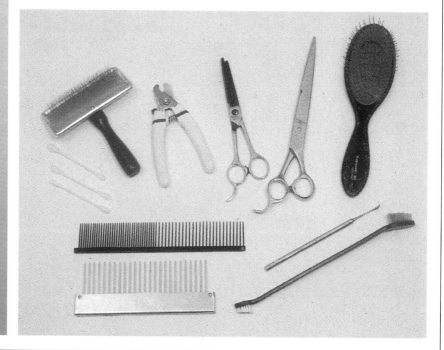

"Tools of the trade." Here are some of the essentials for grooming your Bichon.

This Bichon is fresh from the bath and ready for blow-drying. All Grooming Photographs by Isabelle Francais. Models courtesy of guest author Cliff Steele.

comments on making the most of a potential winner. Cliff has had the lead on numerous successful Bichons who were All-Breed Best in Show, specialty, Non-Sporting Group, and Rating System winners. His highly successful dogs are a credit to our show rings and reflect his talent as they catch one's eye.

To Cliff, my heartfelt appreciation for this interest in this book and for his part in making it a good one.

We shall start off with a rundown of the tools you will need to correctly care for the coat of your Bichon and his proper grooming. At the head of the list comes the grooming table, which you will soon come to consider an invaluable investment for both home use and, if they are in your plans for the future, at the dog shows. Here is where you groom your dog, working on his coat, nails, and ears. Here is also where you can "park" him when ready for the show ring, where he can keep tidy with every hair in place, and relax under your watchful eye until time for judging. Wherever you are with your dog this table will be useful, so make it one of your first investments. They are rubber-topped for the dog's sure footing, have folding legs so they fit out of the way neatly flattened when not in use, and come in a variety of sizes in accordance with your breed. They should be equipped with an arm, from which hangs a noose that slips over the dog's head to keep him tethered to avoid unexpected departures from the table.

For the proper grooming of your Bichon, you will need some carefully selected, high-quality tools. Select them with care and purchase only the best in quality. Remember that the true "bargain" is the one that gives the best service. Thus it is more sensible to choose tools that are easy to work with of a trusted known brand rather than those of lowest cost, which may never give satisfaction. You will need these items as you start plans for your Bichons who include a show career:

Hair dryer (standard type)

Small pin brush

Slicker brush
Greyhound comb (steel)
Nail clippers or electric grinder or both

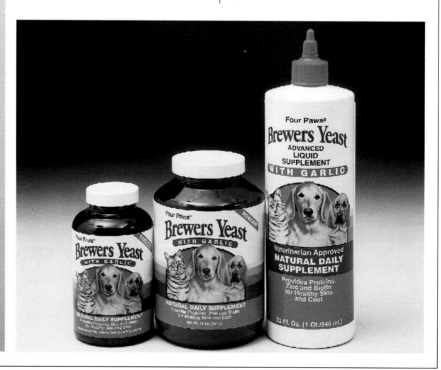

Tooth scaler

Hemostats

Two pairs of top-quality scissors, one blunt-tipped (which you should examine carefully for a comfortable feeling in your hand and smooth easy operation)

You will also need cotton swabs, a wash cloth, and large white (so color cannot bleed on white dog) Turkish towels for blotting excess water following bath and for spreading under the dog on the grooming table.

Around two months old is not too early an age to begin accustoming your Bichon puppy to the fact that his beautiful coat, unique in appearance and an important characteristic of the breed, will need care throughout his lifetime. Gentle brushing (always lifting the hair up and away

Putting powder in the ears after cleaning them. Your Bichon's ears should be cleaned and checked on a weekly basis.

from the body) can be done in the beginning with a light touch on the brush, holding the puppy in your lap. As he matures you will advance him to the grooming table. Puppies started young take grooming as a matter of course, soon learning to lie quietly on first one side then the other, and the rest of the routine, as time progresses.

As the puppy coat grows, it is important to set the course for the future, "shaping" the baby's coat to encourage an even, full coat on the mature dog. Long, scraggly hairs should be snipped to an even length with the overall coat as they appear (called

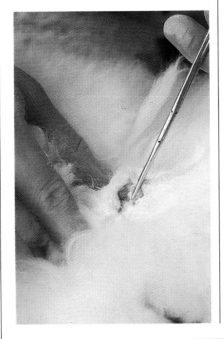

Using a hemoscope to pull hair from the ears. It is necessary to clear away any hairs within your Bichon's ear canal, as they are a prime cause of ear scratching and infection.

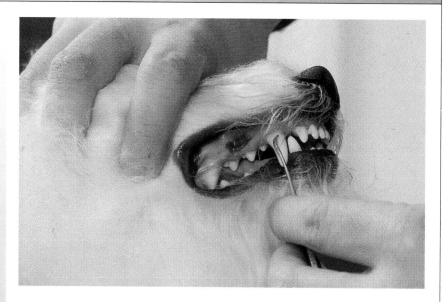

Cleaning the teeth using a scaler. If you are not yet familiar with this procedure, have your vet clean your dog's teeth as you observe and receive instruction at the same time.

"tipping"). In the long run this will make the difference between a beautifully smooth, full, well-rounded "powder puff" coat and one that is uneven and looks unkempt.

That the hair on a baby Bichon is trained to stand out correctly is of tremendous importance. Do not hesitate to cut back the Bichon's coat to a proper length of shortness, if necessary, in training the coat to stand out correctly and to avoid any tendency for it to part even in a youngster! Parting is extremely undesirable in Bichons as it indicates too soft a coat, so keep the baby's coat to a length avoiding this. Better that your Bichon's puppy coat be scissored back to only an inch or slightly more in length than that it become longer and fall into a part

prior to development of the mature density of texture.

Proper care of a Bichon's coat involves a thorough brushing every other day, not terribly big a job when one considers the smallness of the dog! Being a breed that does not shed, extra care is necessary to assist removal of dead hair, which if neglected can quickly become tangled into the live coat. Dead tangled hair can cause serious matting and lead to skin irritation, scratching due to discomfort to the mat, and then hot spots.

It is amazing the speed with which neglected tangling can form into a mat, so do yourself and the dog a favor by making every effort to forestall this. Catch tangles early and correct them with gentle, careful separation of the involved hairs with your fingers and comb, working loose a few hairs at a time. This is definitely one of the areas in which to forestall is far easier than to correct! If a mat is large and stubborn, and the above mentioned manner of loosening the hairs impossible, you might try cutting a slit into the middle of the matted hair with your blunt-tipped scissors and then attempt with comb and fingers to gently remove it. Should all this fail, then there is no alternative other than snipping off the mat carefully and neatly with as little extra hair loss as possible. When this has happened once, I am sure that you will realize the importance of avoiding future recurrences by alert and immediate action! Watch the dog and *notice* and *investigate* excessive

scratching or biting at himself. It may be a mat starting or it may be a flea, each of which demand prompt action for the sake of the coat and for the dog's comfort.

When the brushing and combing have been completed on a full grooming day, you are ready to start with the toenails, teeth, and ears, which should be checked out on a weekly basis. Leave the dog on the grooming table as you continue, with the noose around his neck to avoid any attempt to leave while being worked on. Examine each foot carefully, and keep the nails short. However, be careful to not cut into that pinkish line down the center of each. This line is called the "quick" and will bleed if you go into it with the nail clippers or electric file (nail grinder) and may cause the nail to be sensitive for a day or two afterwards. Watch for the quick before cutting or filing, and stop just ahead of it to shorten the nail. Most dogs dislike having anything done to their feet, so be prepared for a struggle, and if possible have someone hold the dog for you if there is a problem. Should a nail inadvertently be made to bleed, a touch of styptic powder applied with the

In order to groom your Bichon Frise you will need different grooming instruments. Grooming kits are available at your local pet store. Photo courtesy of Wahl Clipper.

finger to the nail tip will stop it with one or two applications immediately.

Different dogs have different reactions to the nail shortening "tools." There are some who hate the electric file, or are terrified by the noise, so you will need to experiment a bit to find out which works best. The grinder (file) does a nice smooth finish to the nail-tip, which is not always the case with the nail clippers. Perhaps it

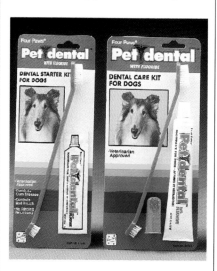

Using pet dental products as part of your dog's oral hygiene care will help fight plaque, reduce tarter buildup and control unpleasant breath. Photo courtesy of Four Paws.

would work out best with those dogs to actually "do" them with the nail clipper, then finish off with a stroke of the grinder to smooth over any rough spots.

Dog owners over the years have become increasingly aware of the dental problems of their canine friends. Nowadays it is quite the custom to brush their teeth using a soft toothbrush, either dry

or with a touch of toothpaste now available for dogs where you buy your pet supplies.

Teeth should be inspected frequently if yours is, or will be, a show dog. It is important that his "pearly whites" will be that for the judge. Look carefully at the teeth, raising the lips front and side, opening the jaws to see inside. Any spots of yellow tartar must be gently removed with the scraper, taking care not to use too heavy a touch. If you are not yet familiar with doing so, have your veterinarian clean the teeth as you observe and receive instruction at the same time. The tooth scraping and brushing will also prove a boon in avoiding bad breath, and are as important to the dental health of a pet as a show dog.

The ears should, on a weekly basis, come in for their share of attention, too, during your grooming procedure. Bichon ears should be examined frequently for a strong odor or any accumulation of brown ear wax, either of which usually indicates an infection or ear mites. If you notice your dog frequently shaking his head, or holding the head to one side, check his ears as this can also indicate a

Choose from a variety of ear care products from cleaners to remedies for proper ear hygiene. Photo courtesy of Four Paws.

problem. Clean ear thoroughly and carefully with a product made expressly for canine ears, using cotton swabs to remove the wax. It is also necessary with Bichons to clear away any hairs within the ear canal as they are a prime cause of ear scratching and infection. Do this by grasping each offending hair firmly with a blunt tweezer, fingers, or the hemoscope and removing with a short, quick jerk. Lightly dust the ear when finished with powder. Watch the ear for any further indication of a problem, in which case it should be examined and treated by your veterinarian.

Your Bichon should be bathed in a sink or small tub of appropriate size for him to stand comfortably. A shampoo hose is needed for wetting him down thoroughly. The best products suitable for bathing a Bichon can be found at your local pet store. Also you will find, at

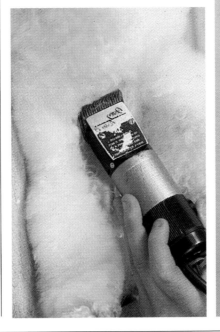

Shaving the belly with electric clippers to create a neat underline.

Combing out the leg. A narrow-toothed comb should be used on the legs and feet.

your supplier, various shampoo products made especially for white dogs that likewise do their work well. Whatever the shampoo, it is of *utmost importance* that the coat be *thoroughly rinsed.* Remember that the least trace of the soap or shampoo that remains in the coat can cause itching, scratching, and eventual hot spots, so beware!

Wash the coat with a gentle squeezing motion, working up a good lather. Some groomers like to give a second soaping, others feel that once is sufficient. When you are certain that the coat is absolutely soap-free, apply the coat conditioner (or cream rinse), with a generous amount for the tail. Again,

opinion is divided on whether or not to rinse out the conditioner. Some say "yes" while others disagree. Consult the directions on the container, then decide. Common sense says that it is more beneficial if allowed to remain, while there is also the opinion that rinsing it out lightly is best.

When the dog has been completely rinsed, is free of soap, and the conditioner attended to, lift him from the tub onto a clean white towel spread over the top of his grooming table. Now starts the period of drying and trimming so important to the overall correctness and beauty of your Bichon when the grooming is complete.

Enhancement of the "powder puff" appearance

must be worked for by using the blow-dry method and constant brushing throughout the process. Teach the dog, from puppyhood, to make himself comfortable on the grooming table, lying first on one side, then the other, for each to be done, then either on his stomach or standing for the back. Work from the head back, brushing with an outward, skin-to-tip-of-hair stroke, entirely up and out from the skin to create that characteristic powder puff!

Right here seems an ideal place to repeat the requirements of the 1988 Standard of Points of the Bichon Frise Club of America regarding the coat. It reads:

"The texture of the coat is of utmost importance. The undercoat is soft and dense, the outercoat of a coarser and curlier texture. The combination of the two gives a soft, but substantial feel to the coat which is similar to plush or velvet, and when patted immediately springs back. When bathed and brushed, it stands off the body, creating an overall powder puff appearance. A wiry coat is not desirable. A limp, silky coat that lies down, or a lack of undercoat are very serious faults."

And on the subject of trimming, the standard continues:

"The coat is trimmed to reveal the natural outline of the body. It is rounded off from any direction, and never cut so short as to create an overly trimmed or squared off appearance. The furnishings of the head, beard, moustache, ears, and tail are left longer. The longer head hair is trimmed to create

Combing out the underchest. Hold the comb so that the teeth point towards you, always raising the hair out from the skin.

an overall rounded impression. The topline is trimmed to appear level. The coat is long enough to maintain the powder puff look which is characteristic of the breed."

As he prepares to start the trimming procedure for us, Cliff Steel reminds us that "every Bichon must be trimmed as an individual dog in accordance with its own conformation and proportions." Study your dog, compare to the standard and to a photo or two of outstanding Bichons which you especially admire and keep these handy as you work.

Watching Cliff do it, the trimming seems quite simple. But do not be

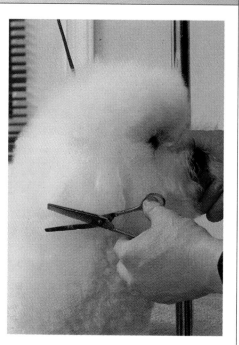

fooled! It is actually a difficult job in the beginning as one learns, and it is simply Cliff's expertise that makes it seem easy. Do not be discouraged, however, if at first you find this far from the case. It takes practice, an eye for balance, and natural talent to turn out a correct grooming job. But one can learn and will do so as time progresses. Never mind, in the beginning, an error or two.

Bichon hair grows quickly, so your mistakes will fill in faster than you might have anticipated. If you have a dog other than the one you are planning to show soon, it is a smart idea to

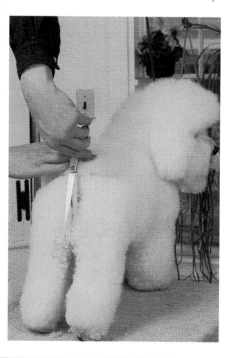

practice the technique on that one until you have had a chance to gain confidence. Remember, too, that you should evaluate and plan your procedure specifically for each individual dog in accordance with that individual's physical characteristics.

When the Bichon is thoroughly dry *(important)* by the brush and blow-dry method, the tendency to curl that is natural to Bichons should have disappeared from view. But the dog needs to have been dried very thoroughly or the inclination towards this curliness may take over, which you do not wish to have happen. It is the blow-dry accompanied by constant careful brushing

Trimming above the eyes. Please exercise extreme care in cutting away the hair around the eyes, use blunt-tipped scissors only.

that "sets" the powder-puff correctly. You will notice the difference promptly if you permit the dog to dry on its own without the brush and blow-dry method. If you find as you proceed that the coat on which you are *not* working is drying too quickly on its own, dampen it slightly as you go along with water from a spray bottle. It will not look right when finished unless the coat was damp when started but thoroughly dry from the brush and blower when done. Work on a small area at a time, lifting the hair with your pin brush as you proceed. Final touches when the job is finished should be done with the slicker brush.

When the Bichon's bath

Trimming the chest. Remember, the coat should never be cut so short as to create an overly trimmed or squared-off appearance.

has been completed, and he has been dried thoroughly as described above, comb him out carefully, dealing with any tangles that may have escaped you and now appear. *(Wide teeth of the comb on the body and the head; narrow teeth on the legs and feet.)* A useful "tip" is that the comb should be held so that the teeth point towards you, always raising the hair out from the skin.

You should now be ready to start scissoring. Do so at the feet, carefully trimming between the pads for the elimination of excess hair. This makes for better traction, and enables the dog to move along smoothly without fear of slipping. The feet should be neatly shaped and free of straggling hairs. Use the blunt scissors, being careful as you do so.

As you scissor the dog have the thought constantly in mind that your goal is the look of a round powder puff, or a series of them. *Frequently* as you work, fluff out the fur with your comb always away from the body. Work slowly in the beginning, and keep in mind that you can always take more off if, when you run the comb through, doing so seems appropriate. A hint that I always suggest when speaking of learning to present a dog well in the show ring is to work in front of a mirror so you can see what is happening on the side toward the judge. That applies as well to grooming as to posing the dog, so do try it.

If you have a dog on which to work who is in show coat and trimmed accordingly, starting on him would be most helpful as you can simply stay within the original pattern already set when you do the dog for the first time. Valuable practice and extremely helpful in learning how it is done!

The photographs accompanying this chapter are the ones especially made for the purpose, and, along with their captions should be carefully studied and referred to as you work.

The furnishings of the head, beard, moustache, ears, and tail should be left longer and trimmed to create an overall rounded appearance.

The finished product—all groomed, beautiful, and ready for the show ring!

Remember the importance of *never* making a move that will flatten out any part of the coat's puffiness. Remember to stop and fluff out the hair as you work, evaluating carefully the effect being created and the even, smooth appearance of the finished picture. You must create smooth, well-proportioned "powder puffs" that must never appear lopsided or poorly shaped. The legs must be equally perfectly shaped cylinders ending in the neatly shaped feet. All parts of the dog need to be well-rounded for that top-quality winner look. Learn to snip a few times then fluff with a comb as that will help to catch anything which may not be turning out correctly.

Your pet Bichon, who may also be your retired show dog, will look very smart and attractive in a shorter, easier-to-keep style than the regularly desired show coat, which should measure about two inches in length. Pets look adorable in a shorter coat, say measuring about one inch in length, and the care of this will be easier to manage with less work on a weekly basis. A couple of brushings a week should keep the shorter coat in good shape, and it is generally agreed that pet Bichons look jaunty and stylish done in this manner. But for the show ring, the two-inch length is a "must."

The Making of a Show Dog

If you have decided to become a show dog exhibitor, you have accepted a very real and very exciting challenge. The groundwork has been accomplished with the selection of your future show prospect. If you have purchased a puppy, it is

At the Enfant Specialty Match in August 1971, *Ch. Jeannine Chez Rivage d'Ami, CD*, handled by Gus Temmel wins Best Adult in Match.

assumed that you have gone through all the proper preliminaries concerning good care, which should be the same if the puppy is a pet or future show dog, with a few added precautions for the latter.

GENERAL CONSIDERATIONS

Remember the importance of keeping your future winner in trim, top condition. Since you want him neither too fat nor too thin, his appetite for his proper diet should be guarded, and children and guests should not be permitted to constantly feed him "goodies." The best treat of all is a small wad of raw ground beef or a packaged dog treat. To be avoided are ice cream, cake, cookies, potato chips, and other fattening items which will cause the dog to put on weight and may additionally spoil his appetite for the proper, nourishing, well-balanced diet so essential to good health and condition.

The importance of temperament and showmanship cannot possibly be overestimated. They have put many a mediocre dog across, while lack of them can ruin the career of an otherwise outstanding specimen. From the day your dog joins your family, socialize him. Keep him accustomed to being with people and to being handled by people. Encourage your friends and relatives to "go over" him as the judges will in the ring so this will not seem a strange and upsetting experience.

Ch. Rank's Eddie, sired by Frostie Muffin ex Rank's Treasure, was one of the leading early Bichons in the country, the first to finish championship following the breed's admission to AKC competition. He was the first Bichon to place in the Westminster Non-Sporting Group after winning the breed there in 1974. Owned by Robert A. Koeppel of New York, and faultlessly handled by Richard Bauer with whom he is pictured here.

Practice showing his "bite" (the manner in which his teeth meet) quickly and deftly. It is quite simple to slip the lips apart with your fingers, and the puppy should be willing to accept this from you or the judge without struggle.

Some judges prefer that the exhibitors display the dog's bite and other mouth features themselves. These are the considerate ones, who do not wish to chance the spreading of possible infection from dog to dog with their hands on each one's mouth—a courtesy particularly appreciated in these days of virus epidemics. But the old-fashioned judges still persist in doing it themselves, so the dog should be ready for either possibility.

Take your future show dog with you in the car, thus accustoming him to

Ch. Sumarco Aloofee Top Gun handled by David Roberts to a Best in Show victory.

riding so that he will not become carsick on the day of a dog show. He should associate pleasure and attention with going in the car, van, or motor home. Take him where it is crowded: downtown, to the shops, everywhere you go that dogs are permitted. Make the expeditions fun for him by frequent petting and words of praise; do not just ignore him as you go about your errands.

Do not overly shelter your future show dog. Instinctively you may want to keep him at home where he is safe from germs or danger. This can be foolish on two counts. The first reason is that a puppy kept away from other dogs builds up no natural

immunity against all the things with which he will come in contact at dog shows, so it is wiser to keep him up-to-date on all protective shots and then let him become accustomed to being among dogs and dog owners. Also, a dog who is never among strange people, in strange places, or among strange dogs may grow up with a shyness or timidity of spirit that will cause you real problems as his show career draws near.

Keep your show prospect's coat in immaculate condition with frequent grooming and daily brushing. When bathing is necessary, use a mild dog shampoo or whatever the breeder of your puppy may suggest. Several of the brand-name products do an excellent job. Be sure to rinse thoroughly so as not to risk skin irritation by traces of soap left behind, and protect against soap entering the eyes by a drop of castor oil in each before you lather up. Use warm water (be sure it is not uncomfortably hot or chillingly cold) and a good spray. Make certain you allow your dog to dry thoroughly in a warm, draft-free area (or outdoors, if it is warm and sunny) so that he doesn't catch cold. Then proceed to groom him to perfection.

This little dog is *Ch. Gaylor's Mr. Magic of Glen Elfred*, owned by Gail Antetomaso and Laurie Scarpa famous for his correct action. Handled by Patty Jenner.

A show dog's teeth must be kept clean and free of tartar. Hard dog biscuits can help toward this, but if tartar accumulates, see that it is removed promptly by your veterinarian. Bones for chewing are not suitable for show dogs as they tend to damage and wear down the tooth enamel.

Assuming that you will be handling the dog yourself, or even if he will be professionally handled, a few moments each day of dog show routine is important. Practice setting him up as you have seen the exhibitors do at the shows you've attended, and teach him to hold this position once you have him stacked to your satisfaction. Make the learning period pleasant by being firm but lavish in your praise when he responds correctly. Teach him to gait at your side at a moderate rate on a loose lead. When you have mastered the basic essentials at home, then hunt out and join a training class for future work. Training classes are sponsored by show-giving clubs in many areas, and their popularity is steadily increasing. If you have no other way of locating one, perhaps your veterinarian would know of one through some of his other clients; but if you are sufficiently aware of the dog show world to want a show dog, you will probably be personally acquainted with other people who will share information of this type with you.

Accustom your show dog to being in a crate (which you should be doing with a pet dog as well). He should relax in his crate at the shows "between times" for his own well being and safety.

FIRST
BROOD BITCH

BICHON FRISE
CLUB OF AMERICA
MAY
1991
DAVE ASHBEY

MATCH SHOWS

Your show dog's initial experience in the ring should be in match show competition. This type of event is intended as a learning experience for both the dog and the exhibitor. You will not feel embarrassed or out of place no matter how poorly your puppy may behave or how inept your attempts at handling may be, as you will find others there with the same type of problems. The important thing is that you get the puppy out and into a show ring where the two of you can practice together and learn the ropes.

Only on rare occasions is it necessary to make match show entries in advance, and even those with a pre-entry policy will usually accept entries at the door as well. Thus you need not plan several weeks ahead,

In really tough competition provided by no less than six competing dams with their offspring, *Dove Cote's Crackerjack* won the class at the 1991 Bichon Frise Club of America National Specialty with her two daughters, *Ch.Pillow Talk's Kissin' Fool* and*Ch. Pillow Talk's Special K*. Both are sired by Ch. Dove Cote's Mr. Magoo, ROM. Bred by Lori and Tracy Kornfeld, Ridgefield, Connecticut.

Above: Westminster Kennel Club Dog Show, the world's largest benching show. Resting in the benching area behind the scenes, and awaiting his turn in the ring is *M. and A.'s Count D'Amour* owned by Michael and Toni Ambrosia, New Jersey. Lower right: *Ch. Dove-Cote's Valentine Heidi* with handler Kathy Kirk. Owned by Irene B. and Joseph R. Libby, Enfield, Connecticut.

as is the case with point shows, but can go when the mood strikes you. Also there is a vast difference in the cost, as match show entries only cost a few dollars while entry fees for the point shows may be over fifteen dollars, an amount none of us needs to waste until we have some idea of how the puppy will behave or how much more pre-show training is needed.

Match shows are frequently judged by professional handlers who, in addition to making the awards, are happy to help new exhibitors with comments and advice on their puppies and their presentation of them. Avail yourself of all these opportunities before heading out to the sophisticated world of the point shows.

POINT SHOWS

Point shows are essentially an American

and Continental convention. The process and classes in England are entirely different. Entries for American Kennel Club point shows must be made in advance. This must be done on an official entry blank of the show-giving club. The entry must then be filed either personally or by mail with the show superintendent or the show secretary (if the event is being run by the club members alone and a superintendent has not been hired, this information will appear on the premium list) in time to reach its destination prior to the published closing date or filling of the quota. These entries must be made

carefully, must be signed by the owner of the dog or the owner's agent (your professional handler), and must be accompanied by the entry fee; otherwise they will not be accepted. Remember that it is not when the entry leaves your hands that counts, but the date of arrival at its destination. If you are relying on the mails, which are not always dependable, get the entry off well before the deadline to avoid disappointment.

A dog must be entered at a dog show in the name of the actual owner at the time of the entry closing date of that specific show. If a registered dog has been acquired by a new owner, it must be entered in the

name of the new owner in any show for which entries close after the date of acquirement, regardless of whether the new owner has or has not actually received the registration certificate indicating that the dog is recorded in his name. State on the entry form whether or not transfer application has been mailed to the American Kennel Club, and it goes without saying that the latter should be attended to promptly when you purchase a registered dog.

In filling out your entry blank, type, print, or write clearly, paying particular attention to the spelling of names, correct registration numbers, and so on. Also, if there is more than one variety in your breed, be sure to indicate into which category your dog is being entered.

The **Puppy Class** is for dogs or bitches who are six months of age and under twelve months and who are

Left: *La Joli Bibi de Reenroy* by Mon Ami du Pic Four ex No No Nanette de Reenroy. Owned by Celeste Fleishman, Bibi was a consistant winner in miscellaneous classes, in the early AKC days of the Bichon.

Below: *Ch. Azara Zardin*, was the first import to the United States from Azara Kennels in Australia. Zardin was best of Winners at Westminster in 1986 with Joe Waterman handling for owner Mrs. Celeste Fleischman of Gwynedd Valley, Pennsylvania, and went on to become an important and famous winner and producer in the United States.

BEST OF
BREED

THE WESTMINSTER
KENNEL CLUB
FEBRUARY 13-14, 1978

ASHBEY

Ch. Larica's Ondine of Hillwood won the 1978 Best of Breed award at Westminster with handler Richard Bauer. Owned by Ellen Iverson. Photo courtesy of David Roberts.

not champions. The age of a dog shall be calculated up to and inclusive of the first day of a show. For example, the first day a dog whelped on January 1st is eligible to compete in a Puppy Class at a show is July 1st of the same year; and he may continue to compete in Puppy Classes up to and including a show on December 31 of the same year, but he is *not* eligible to compete in a Puppy Class at a show held on or after January 1 of the following year.

The Puppy Class is the first one in which you should enter your puppy. In it a certain allowance will be made for the fact that they *are* puppies, thus an immature dog or one displaying less than perfect showmanship will be less severely penalized than, for instance, would be the case in Open. It is also quite likely that others in the class will be suffering from these problems, too. When you enter a puppy, be sure to check the classification with care, as some shows divide their Puppy Class into a 6-9 months old section and a 9-12 months old section.

The **Novice Class** is for dogs six months of age and over, whelped in the United States or Canada, who *prior to the official closing date for entries* have *not* won three first prizes in the Novice Class, any first prize at all in the Bred-by-Exhibitor, American-bred, or Open Classes, or one or more points toward championship. The provisions for this class are confusing to many people, which is probably the reason exhibitors do not enter in it more frequently. A dog may win any number of first prizes in the Puppy Class and still retain his eligibility for Novice. He may place second, third, or fourth not only in Novice on an unlimited number of occasions, but also in Bred-by-Exhibitor, American-bred and Open and still remain eligible for Novice. But he may no longer be shown in Novice when he has won three blue ribbons in that class, when he has won even one blue ribbon in either Bred-by-Exhibitor, American-bred, or Open, or when he has won a single championship point.

In determining whether or not a dog is eligible for the Novice Class, keep in mind the fact that previous wins are calculated according to the official published date for closing of entries, not by the date on which you may actually have made the entry. So if in the interim, between the time you made the entry and the official closing date, your dog makes a win causing him to become ineligible for Novice, change your class *immediately* to another for which he will be eligible,

Ch. Pillow Talk's Kissin' Fool, with handler Cliff Steele and her son *Pillow Talk's Judges Choice*, with Lori Kornfeld. Owned and bred by Tracy and Lori Kornfeld.

preferably either Bred-by-Exhibitor or American-bred. To do this, you must contact the show's superintendent or secretary, at first by telephone to save time and then in writing to confirm it. The Novice Class always seems to have the fewest entries of any class, and therefore it is a splendid "practice ground" for you and your young dog while you are getting the "feel" of being in the ring.

Bred-by-Exhibitor Class is for dogs whelped in the United States or, if individually registered in the American Kennel Club Stud Book, for dogs whelped in Canada who are six months of age or older, are not champions, and are owned wholly or in part by the person or by the spouse of the person who was the breeder or one of the breeders of record. Dogs entered in this class must be handled in the class by an owner or by a member of the immediate family of the owner. Members of an immediate family for this purpose are husband, wife, father, mother, son, daughter, brother, or sister. This is the class which is really the "breeders' showcase," and the one which breeders should enter with particular pride to show off their achievements.

The **American-bred Class** is for all dogs excepting champions, six months of age or older, who were whelped in the United States by reason of a mating which took place in the United States.

The **Open Class** is for any dog six months of age

or older (this is the only restriction for this class). Dogs with championship points compete in it, dogs who are already champions are eligible to do so, dogs who are imported can be entered, and, of course, American-bred dogs compete in it. This class is, for some strange reason, the favorite of exhibitors who are "out to win." They rush to enter their pointed dogs in it, under the false impression that by doing so they assure themselves of greater attention from the judges. This really is not so, and some people feel that to enter in one of the less competitive classes, with a better chance of winning it and thus

day in one of these classes is eligible to compete for Winners, and every dog who has been a blue-ribbon winner in one of them and not defeated in another, should he have been entered in more than one class (as occasionally happens), *must* do so.

Braymar Bali Hai heads this line with five of her 11 champion offspring helping her to win the Brood Bitch Class at the San Diego

earning a second opportunity of gaining the judge's approval by returning to the ring in the Winners Class, can often be a more effective strategy.

One does not enter the **Winners Class.** One earns the right to compete in it by winning first prize in Puppy, Novice, Bred-by-Exhibitor, American-bred, or Open. No dog who has been defeated on the same

Following the selection of the Winners Dog or the Winners Bitch, the dog or bitch receiving that award leaves the ring. Then the dog or bitch who placed second in that class, unless previously beaten by another dog or bitch in another class at the same show, re-enters the ring to compete against the remaining first-prize winners for Reserve. The

Specialty in 1982. Bali Hai was bred and owned by Roberta Rothman, and co-owned by Barbara Stubbs.

Sara de Staramour, by Ch. Azara Zardin ex Balle de Neige de Staramour, is one of the current Bichons belonging to Mrs. Celeste Fleishman, Staramour Kennels. Shown by Carol Nock.

latter award indicates that the dog or bitch selected for it is standing "in reserve" should the one who received Winners be disqualified or declared ineligible through any technicality when the awards are checked at the American Kennel Club. In that case, the one who placed Reserve is moved up to Winners, at the same time receiving the appropriate championship points.

Winners Dog and Winners Bitch are the awards which carry points toward championship with them. The points are based on the number of dogs or bitches actually in competition, and the points are scaled one through five, the latter being the greatest number available to any

one dog or bitch at any one show. Three-, four-, or five-point wins are considered majors. In order to become a champion, a dog or bitch must have won two majors under two different judges, plus at least one point from a third judge, and the additional points necessary to bring the total to fifteen. When your dog has gained fifteen points as described above, a championship certificate will be issued to you, and your dog's name will be published in the champions of record list in the *Pure-Bred Dogs/American Kennel Gazette*, the official publication of the American Kennel Club.

The scale of championship points for each breed is worked out by the American Kennel Club and reviewed annually, at

Ch. Stardom's Niki de Staramour, ROM by Ch. Titan de Wanarbry ex Jean Rank's Crystal, pictured winning Group One placement in 1974. Owned by Mrs. Celeste Fleishman, Staramour Kennels.

which time the number required in competition may be either changed (raised or lowered) or remain the same. The scale of championship points for all breeds is published annually in the May issue of the *Gazette*, and the current ratings for each breed within that area are published in every show catalog.

When a dog or bitch is adjudged Best of Winners, its championship points are, for that show, compiled on the basis of which sex had the greater number of points. If there are two points in dogs and four in bitches and the dog goes Best of Winners, then *both* the dog and the bitch are awarded an equal number of points, in this case four. Should the

Winners Dog or the Winners Bitch go on to win Best of Breed or Best of Variety, additional points are accorded for the additional dogs and bitches defeated by so doing, provided, of course, that there were entries specifically for Best of Breed competition or specials, as these specific entries are generally called.

If your dog or bitch takes Best of Opposite Sex after going Winners, points are credited according to the number of the same sex defeated in both the regular classes and Specials competition. If Best of Winners is also won, then whatever additional points for each of these awards are available will be credited. Many a one- or two-point win has grown into a major in this manner.

Moving further along, should your dog win its **Variety Group** from the classes (in other words, if it has taken either Winners Dog or Winners Bitch), you then receive points based on the greatest number of points awarded to any member of any breed included within that Group during that show's competition. Should the day's winning also include Best in Show, the same rule of thumb applies, and your dog or bitch receives the highest number of points awarded to any other dog of any breed at that event.

Best of Breed competition consists of the Winners Dog and the Winners Bitch, who automatically compete on the strength of those awards, in addition to whatever dogs and bitches have been entered specifically for this class for which champions of record are eligible. Since July 1980, dogs who, according to their owner's records, have completed the requirements for a championship after the closing of entries for the show (but whose championships are unconfirmed) may be transferred from one of the regular classes to the Best of Breed competition, provided this transfer is made by the show superintendent or show secretary *prior to the start of any judging at the show.*

This has proved an extremely popular new rule, as under it a dog can finish on Saturday and then be transferred and compete as a Special on Sunday. It must be emphasized that *the change must be made prior to the start of any part of the day's judging, not for just your individual breed.*

In the United States, Best of Breed winners are entitled to compete in the Variety Group which includes them. This is not mandatory; it is a privilege which exhibitors value. (In Canada, Best of Breed winners *must* compete in the Variety Group or they lose any points already won.) The dogs winning *first* in each of the seven Variety Groups *must* compete for Best in Show. Missing the opportunity of taking your dog in for competition in its Group is foolish, as it is there where the general public is most likely to notice your breed and become interested in learning about it.

Non-regular classes are sometimes included at the all-breed shows, and they are almost invariably

Top: The top-winning Ch. Beau Cheval's Red Roses handled by David Roberts for a Group One under the author in 1995. Casper is by Ch. Beau Cheval's Ms. Mums ex Ch. Ladywood's Favorite Beau. Owners, David Ruml and Mrs. I. F. Zimmerman. *Bottom:* Ch. Windstar's The Banjo Man, "Strummer," bred by Mrs. Estelle Kellerman has been a consistent winner for owner Robert Koeppel.

included at specialty shows. These include Stud Dog Class and Brood Bitch Class, which are judged on the basis of the quality of the two offspring accompanying the sire or dam. The quality of the latter two is beside the point and should not be considered by the judge; it is the youngsters who count, and the quality of *both* are to be averaged to decide which sire or dam is the best and most consistent producer. Then there is the Brace Class (which, at all-breed shows, moves up to Best Brace in each Variety Group and then Best Brace in Show) which is judged on the similarity and evenness of appearance of the two brace members. In other words, the two dogs should look like identical twins in size, color, and conformation and should move together almost as a single dog, one person handling with precision and ease. The same applies to the Team Class competition, except that four dogs are involved and, if necessary, two handlers.

The Veterans Class is for the older dog, the minimum age of whom is seven years. This class is judged on the quality of the dogs, as the winner competes in Best of Breed competition and has, on a respectable number of occasions, been known to take that top award. So the point is *not* to pick out the oldest dog, as some judges seem to believe,

The outstanding and successful star, *Ch. Beau Monde Top Banana*, handled by Joe Waterman for owner Jeff Bennett.

Ch. Camelot's Brassy Nickel, CDX winning Best in Show with handler Clifford Steel. Brassy has been an important winning competitor at Eastern shows throughout his career and has numerous title-holders to his credit as a sire. Owned by Pam Goldman.

but the best specimen of the breed, exactly as in the regular classes.

Then there are Sweepstakes and Futurity Stakes sponsored by many Specialty clubs, sometimes as part of their regular Specialty shows and sometimes as separate events on an entirely different occasion. The difference between the two stakes is that Sweepstakes entries usually include dogs from six to eighteen months of age with entries made at the same time as the others for the show, while for a Futurity the entries are bitches nominated when bred and the individual puppies entered at or shortly following their birth.

JUNIOR SHOWMANSHIP COMPETITION

If there is a youngster in your family between the ages of ten and sixteen, there is no better or more rewarding hobby than becoming an active participant in Junior Showmanship. This is a marvelous activity for young people. It teaches responsibility, good sportsmanship, the fun of competition where one's own skills are the deciding factor of success, proper care of a pet, and how to socialize with other young folks. Any youngster may experience the thrill of emerging from the ring a winner and the satisfaction of a good job well done.

Entry in Junior Showmanship Classes is open to any boy or girl who is at least ten years old and under seventeen years old on the day of the show. The Novice Junior Showmanship Class is open to youngsters who have not already won, at the time the entries close, three firsts in this class. Youngsters who have won three firsts in Novice may compete in the Open Junior Showmanship Class. Any junior handler who wins his third first-place award in Novice may participate in the Open Class at the same show, provided that the Open Class has at least one other junior handler entered and competing in it that day. The Novice and Open Classes may be divided into Junior and Senior Classes. Youngsters between the ages of ten and twelve, inclusively, are eligible for

the Junior division; and youngsters between thirteen and seventeen, inclusively, are eligible for the Senior division.

Any of the foregoing classes may be separated into individual classes for boys and for girls. If such a division is made, it must be so indicated on the premium list. The premium list also indicates the prize for Best Junior Handler, if such a prize is being offered at the show. Any youngster who wins a first in any of the regular classes may enter the competition for this prize, provided the youngster has been undefeated in any other Junior Showmanship Class at that show.

Junior Showmanship Classes, unlike regular conformation classes in which the quality of the dog is judged, are judged solely on the skill and ability of the junior handling the dog. Which dog is best is not the point—it is which youngster does the best job with the dog that is under consideration. Eligibility requirements for the dog being shown in Junior Showmanship, and other detailed information, can be found in *Regulations for Junior Showmanship*, available from the American Kennel Club.

A junior who has a dog that he or she can enter in

The Junior Showmanship Competition at Westminster had its first Bichon Frise placed in 1975. Here *Ch. Beau Monde Works D'Art Witty* takes third place handled by Wendy Kellerman.

Daniel Ruggles, at 12 years of age, is pictured with *Ch. Dove Cote's Pillow Talk T.K.O.* winning Best Jr. Handler at the Bichon Frise Club of America 1992 National Specialty. Daniel was also the #1 ranked Bichon Frise Junior Handler for 1992.

both Junior Showmanship and conformation classes has twice the opportunity for success and twice the opportunity to get into the ring and work with the dog, a combination which can lead to not only awards for expert handling, but also, if the dog is of sufficient quality, for making a conformation champion.

PRE-SHOW PREPARATIONS

Preparation of the items you will need as a dog show exhibitor should not be left until the last moment. They should be planned and arranged several days in advance of the show in order for you to remain calm and relaxed as the countdown starts.

The importance of the crate has already been mentioned and should already be part of your equipment. Of equal importance is the grooming table, which very likely you have also already acquired for use at home. You should take it along with you to the shows, as your dog will need last minute touches before entering the ring. Should you have not yet made this purchase, folding tables with rubber tops are made specifically for this purpose and can be purchased at most dog shows, where concession booths with marvelous assortments of "doggy" necessities are to be found, or at your pet supplier. You

Rivage D'Ami's Richochet Rogue taking points towards championship under the author at a dog show in the 1970s. George Temmel of New York City is the owner.

will also need a sturdy tack box (also available at the dog show concessions) in which to carry your grooming tools and equipment. The latter should include: brushes; combs; scissors; nail clippers; whatever you use for last minute clean-up jobs; cotton swabs; first-aid equipment; and anything you are in the habit of using on the dog, including a leash or two of the type you prefer, some well-cooked and dried-out liver or any of the small packaged "dog treats" for use as bait in the ring, an atomizer in case you wish to dampen your dog's coat when you are preparing him for the ring, and so on. A large turkish

towel to spread under the dog on the grooming table is also useful.

Take a large thermos or cooler of ice, the biggest one you can accommodate in your vehicle, for use by "man and beast." Take a jug of water (there are lightweight, inexpensive ones available at all sporting goods shops) and a water dish. If you plan to feed the dog at the show, or if you and the dog will be away from home more than one day, bring food for him from home so that he will have the type to which he is accustomed.

You may or may not have an exercise pen. While the shows do provide areas for exercise of the dogs, these are among the most likely places to have your dog come in contact with any illnesses which may be going around, and having a pen of your own for your dog's use is excellent protection. Such a pen comes in handy while you're travelling; since it is roomier than a crate, it becomes a comfortable place for your dog to relax and move around in, especially when you're at motels or rest stops. These pens are available at the show concession stands and come in a variety of heights and sizes. A set of "pooper scoopers" should also be part of your equipment, along with a package of plastic bags for cleaning up after your dog.

Bring along folding chairs for the members of your party, unless all of you are fond of standing, as these are almost never provided by the clubs. Have your name stamped on the chairs so that there will be no doubt as to whom the chairs belong. Bring whatever you and your family enjoy for drinks or snacks in a picnic basket or cooler, as show food, in general, is expensive and usually not great. You should always have a pair of boots, a raincoat, and a rain hat with you (they should remain permanently in your vehicle if you plan to attend shows regularly), as well as a sweater, a warm coat, and a change of shoes. A smock or big cover-up apron will assure that you remain tidy as you prepare the dog for the ring. Your overnight case

GROUP 1ST

CENTRAL NEW YORK
KENNEL CLUB, INC.
NOV. 9, 1974

Am. Ch. Titan de Wanarbry was imported from France to join the distinguished Bichons at the Staramour Kennels of Mrs. Celeste Fleishman in Pennsylvania. Titan is by Jimbo of Steren-Vor ex Janitzia des Frimousettes, and is pictured upon the occassion of one of his Group One placements handled by Jane Forsyth.

Ch. Jalwin Just So, by Ch. Devon Viva Poncho ex Ch. Jalwin Journal Illuminato is taking Winners at the Bichon Frise Club of America National Specialty in June 1987.

should include a small sewing kit for emergency repairs, bandaids, headache and indigestion remedies, and any personal products or medications you normally use.

In your car, you should always carry maps of the area where you are headed and an assortment of motel directories. Generally speaking, Holiday Inns have been found to be the

do). Some of the smaller chains welcome pets; the majority of privately-owned motels do not.

Have everything prepared the night before the show to expedite your departure. Be sure that the dog's identification and your judging program and other show information are in your purse or briefcase. If you are taking sandwiches, have them ready. Anything

Breeder/owner, Ann Hearn, Atlanta, Georgia.

nicest about taking dogs. Ramadas and Howard Johnsons generally do so cheerfully (with a few exceptions). Best Western generally frowns on pets (not always, but often enough to make it necessary to find out which

that goes into the car the night before the show will be one thing less to remember in the morning. Decide upon what you will wear and have it out and ready. If there is any question in your mind about what to wear, try on the possibilities before the day of the show; don't risk feeling you may want to change when you see yourself dressed a few moments prior to departure time!

In planning your outfit, make it something simple that will not detract from your dog. Remember that a dark dog silhouettes attractively against a light background and vice-versa. Sport clothes always seem to look best at dog shows, preferably conservative in type and not overly "loud" as you do not want to detract from your dog, who should be the focus of interest at this point. What you wear on your feet is important. Many types of flooring can be hazardously slippery, as can wet grass. Make it a habit to wear rubber soles and low or flat heels in the ring for your own safety, especially if you are showing a dog that likes to move out smartly.

Your final step in pre-show preparation is to leave yourself plenty of time to reach the show that morning. Traffic can get amazingly heavy as one nears the immediate area of the show, finding a parking place can be difficult, and other delays may occur. You'll be in better humor to enjoy the day if your trip to the show is not fraught with panic over fear of not arriving in time!

ENJOYING THE DOG SHOW

From the moment of your arrival at the show until after your dog has been judged, keep foremost in your mind the fact that he is your reason for being there and that he should therefore be the center of your attention. Arrive early enough to have time for those last-minute touches that can make a great difference when he enters the ring. Be sure that he has ample time to exercise and that he attends to

Ch. Miri-Cal's Motet here is finishing title at Westminster Kennel Club 1980 handled by Paul Edwards for owners Ed and Anne Jones, Charles City, Virginia. Motet was among the BFCA top ten of the breed in 1981.

Ch. Glen Elfred's Misty Blue was bred and is owned by Eleanor Grassick, Elmont, New York, for whom Patricia Jenner is handling.

personal matters. A dog arriving in the ring and immediately using it as an exercise pen hardly makes a favorable impression on the judge.

When you reach ringside, ask the steward for your arm-card and anchor it firmly into place on your arm. Make sure that you are where you should be when your class is called. The fact that you have

picked up your arm-card does not guarantee, as some seem to think, that the judge will wait for you. The judge has a full schedule which he wishes to complete on time. Even though you may be nervous, assume an air of calm self-confidence. Remember that this is a hobby to be enjoyed, so approach it in that state of mind. The dog will do better, too, as he will be quick to reflect your attitude.

Always show your dog with an air of pride. If you make mistakes in presenting him, don't worry about it. Next time you will do better. Do not permit the presence of more experienced exhibitors to intimidate you. After all, they, too, were once newcomers.

The judging routine usually starts when the judge asks that the dogs be gaited in a circle around the ring. During this period the judge is watching each dog as it moves, noting style, topline, reach and drive, head and tail carriage, and general balance. Keep your mind and your eye on your dog, moving him at his most becoming gait and keeping your place in line without coming too close to the exhibitor ahead of you. Always keep your dog on

Ch. Glen Elfred's Petite Maid Marion is a multiple Best of Breed winner from the classes. She is the dam of Ch. Gaylon's Mr. Magic. Handled by Patricia Jenner. Owned by Glen Elfred Bichons, Elmont, New York.

the inside of the circle, between yourself and the judge, so that the judge's view of the dog is unobstructed.

Calmly pose the dog when requested to set up for examination. If you are at the head of the line and many dogs are in the class, go all the way to the end of the ring before starting to stack the dog, leaving sufficient space for those behind you to line theirs up as well, as requested by the judge. If you are not at the head of the line but between other exhibitors, leave sufficient space ahead of your dog for the judge to examine him. The dogs should be spaced so that the judge is able to move among them to see them from all angles. In practicing to "set up" or "stack" your dog for the judge's examination, bear in mind the importance of doing so quickly and with dexterity. The judge has a schedule to meet and only a few moments in which to evaluate each dog. You will immeasurably help yours to make a favorable impression if you are able to "get it all together" in a minimum amount of time. Practice at home before a mirror can be a great help toward bringing this about, facing the dog so that you see him from the same side that the judge will and working to make him look right in the shortest length of time.

Listen carefully as the judge describes the manner in which the dog is to be gaited, whether it is straight down and straight back; down the ring, across, and back; or in a triangle. The latter has become the most popular pattern with the majority of judges. "In a triangle"

Ch. Morning Dove's Odelette is pictured winning a Group two placement in August 1991. Sired by Ch. C. and D.'s Samson ex Ch. C. and D.'s Distan Lace N Promise. Owner, Nancy Schmidt, Oshkosh, Wisconsin.

means the dog should move down the outer side of the ring to the first corner, across that end of the ring to the second corner, and then back to the judge from the second corner, using the center of the ring in a diagonal line. Please learn to do this pattern without breaking at each corner to twirl the dog around you, a senseless maneuver that has been noticed on occasion. Judges like to see the dog in an uninterrupted triangle, as they are thus able to get a better idea of the dog's gait.

It is impossible to overemphasize that the gait at which you move your dog is tremendously important and considerable study and thought should be given to the matter. At home, have someone move the dog for you at different speeds so that you can tell which shows him off to best advantage. The most becoming action almost invariably is seen at a moderate gait, head up and topline holding. Do not gallop your dog around the ring or hurry him into a speed atypical of his breed. Nothing being rushed appears at its best; give your dog a chance to move along at his (and the breed's) natural gait. For a dog's action to be judged accurately, that dog should

move with strength and power, but not excessive speed, holding a straight line as he goes to and from the judge.

As you bring the dog back to the judge, stop him a few feet away and be sure that he is standing in a becoming position. Bait him to show the judge an alert expression, using whatever tasty morsel he has been trained to expect for this purpose or, if that works better for you, use a small squeak-toy in your hand. A reminder, please, to those using liver or treats: take them with you when you leave the ring. Do not just drop them on the ground where they will be found by another dog.

When the awards have been made, accept yours graciously, no matter how you actually may feel about it. What's done is done, and arguing with a judge or stomping out of the ring is useless and a reflection on your sportsmanship. Be courteous, congratulate the winner if your dog was defeated, and try not to show your disappointment. By the same token, please be a gracious winner; this, surprisingly, sometimes seems to be still more difficult.

Ch. Jalwin Pattern of Pawmark, daughter of Ch. Norvik's Newscaster ex Ch. Jalwin Illume De Noel, ROM. Owned and bred by Ann Hearn, Atlanta, Georgia.

Judging Bichons

Whether you are interested in evaluating the show quality of a Bichon Frise for your own purposes (such as the selection of one to purchase or grading your homebreds), or eventually as a judge of the breed, the same basic facts apply and will prepare you to recognize and appreciate the correct conformation, balance, movement, and type. The learning process is a continuing one to which time and study bring results. So, the sooner you get started, the more quickly you should learn and the sooner you become an expert.

The standard of the breed is your basic guide. Refer to it frequently as a "refresher." Study it with care, and learn everything it tells you. Do not just learn a series of words verbatim, but the meaning of those words; what they are saying, and their application to actual dogs. Just knowing the words themselves is not enough. What it takes is the recognition of their interpretation as you look at an actual Bichon. Many people know the words but

Bichon breeder/judge Ann Hearn, officer, director and former President of the Bichon Frise Club of America, awarding placement to *Ch.Miri-Cal's Motet* at the 1988 Specialty for Veteran Dogs.

Ch. Beau Monde Regal Rose, owned and handled by Ellen Iverson MacNeille, winning under the highly esteemed judge, William L. Kendrick.

cannot understand their message. That is where the secret lies of correct breed evaluation: in the ability to translate words into the Bichon.

When you are looking at a show Bichon, you should see a well-balanced dog of style and elegance that freely and correctly moves and is strong in true Bichon type. This combination of features makes this dog instantly recognizable to the knowledgeable eye. In the case of the Bichon, the components of type include the correct head and facial features; his distinctive action and carriage as he gaits; his balance; and the wonderful, unique quality of coat; all of which we shall discuss here.

Balance is of utmost importance as one looks at a Bichon, or a group or a class of them. The dog that first attracts your eye should do so owing to his look of "rightness." This translates as every part of the dog being in correct proportion to every other part (i.e., muzzle to skull, head to body, neck to head and body, and length of leg to the dog as a whole). Everything about such a dog looks right as part of the total picture, and thus the dog is truly well balanced.

Study the words of the standard. Study some of the dogs themselves or review the wonderful photos in this book of the world's top winning Bichons.

As you study, you will note that the Bichon muzzle must look neither coarse and heavy nor excessively long. The neck should be of good length and graceful, carrying the head proudly for the desirable elegance, running smoothly into the topline.

The body should be *slightly* longer than the height of the dog at the withers; not so much longer as to make the dog resemble a short-legged terrier breed, nor so short as to make him appear too compact or "leggy." There

Lois Morrow with *Ch. Chaminade Satin Doll*. A fine example of how a good moving Bichon looks in action.

has been tremendous improvement in this area since the early Bichons seen in America, many of whom seemed out of proportion for the length of their legs. Now, I am happy to say, the majority of Bichons we are seeing are, as they should be, correctly proportioned following the words of the standard on the subject. Which gives us as the dog stands, head and tail correctly carried proudly, only a little bit longer than square.

You will soon find (if not already) that a well-made dog will move correctly. Bichon forelegs come straight down from elbow to paw, with a long reach and no crossing or weaving. The hindquarters are muscular and "well let down," which means that there must be good bend of stifle and hock, flexing well with powerful "drive" as the dog travels. Always see a Bichon move straight to and from you and from the side (in judging, having the dogs move individually in a triangle accomplishes this for you) before reaching a decision on him. Bear in mind that his carriage should be jaunty, his head up and tail over the back, and that he should travel in a straight line, not come at you sideways (which is known as "sidetracking"). The action of Bichons

should be judged at a trot, *never* at a gallop.

You will notice as he moves that the Bichon has a *slight* rise over the loin. This should be a hardly perceptible gentle rise, and *never* a roach back or anything even nearly approaching that condition.

Correct head type is

largely dependent on the size, shape, and color of the Bichon eye. This eye should be *large, round,* and either very dark brown or black. The eye is surrounded by a perfect rim of pigmentation known as the "eye halo," which beautifully enhances this feature. A small eye, an oblique eye, or one that is almond-shaped all are objectionable in a Bichon,

A neat and handsome silhouette showing the good balance and quality of *Ch. Gatlon's Mr. Magic of Glenelfred.* Owned by Gail Antetomaso.

Dr. Sam Draper presenting *Ch. Kaleb Paper Doll* with the Best of Winners award at the May 1980 Bichon National Specialty. Owner-handler, Judy Fausset.

as is an eye that bulges. This is an important part of a Bichon's correct type, so do note carefully in going over the dog that there is no break in the dark "halo" and that the eyes are *round* and *dark*.

The color of the Bichon is correctly and preferably pure white. Pale buff, cream, or apricot sometimes appears on ears or on body to a *small* extent, which is tolerable in puppies, but any color exceeding 10% of the entire coat of an adult Bichon is penalized as a fault.

The Bichon's coat is truly his crowning glory; unique, beautiful. A pleasure to look at or touch it instantly tells the world "this dog is a Bichon Frise," for it is unique to this breed only. To the touch, it feels like plush. The appearance it

Dr. Sam Draper presenting *Ch. Kaleb Paper Doll* with the Best of Winners award at the May 1980 Bichon National Specialty. Owner-handler, Judy Fausset.

gives is of a powder puff. It is a source of interest and admiration quickly expressed by all who see it. The coat is actually silky in texture (never harsh nor overly coarse), profuse, and curly, backed by a profuse, thick undercoat. It is never the texture of a Poodle coat, although it, too, stands out from the body. This is attained by brush-drying your Bichon, always from the skin away from the body, plus "tipping" to keep the hair neat and even. It is by *this* means that the powder puff look is attained, *not* by sacrifice of the correct silky texture.

Former standards for Bichons have given far too great leeway in the allowable height for these dogs, which at one period did create a problem regarding size. Oversize can lead to giants if allowed to continue, and really tiny ones can lead to "toyishness." Thus we are very glad that what formerly was considered to be the "ideal" size area, 9½-11½ inches, now has become the size limitation. The two additional inches once allowed was certainly too wide a range for dogs of this size, as American breeders quickly discovered.

This is *Rivage d'Ami's Dynamic Rogue,* owned by Mrs. Helen Temmel, in 1974 winning Best of Breed at the National Specialty in Atlanta under Mrs. James Edward Clark.

Ch. Sandra de la Lande ge Belleville winning a prestigious Best of Opposite Sex award under judge Mary Nelson Stevenson and owner/handler Helen Temmell.

Jeannine Chez Rivage d'Ami, CD winning at Bronx County under breeder/judge Martin Rothman. Owner/handler Helen Temmel.

These enchanting youngsters and highly successful littermates are: *Pillow Talk's Top Flight*, and *Pillow Talk's Top Preference* bred by Tracy and Lori Kornfeld of Ridgefield, Connecticut, pictured with judge Michelle Billings. Shown by David Roberts and Lori Kornfield.

Obedience and Bichons

by Pam Goldman

Obedience has been part of exhibiting Bichons ever since they were recognized by the American Kennel Club. Some of our earliest Champions were also obedience titlists. Ch. Sandra de la Lande de Belleville CD, CDX (in 1973), UD (1976), Bermuda CD, owned by Helen Temmel, earned her first obedience title in 1971 while the breed was still in the Miscellaneous Class, and became a Champion in 1974 between her second and third titles. Ch. Chateau's Idealbo Rivage D'Ami, also owned by Helen Temmel, became the first male titlist in 1972. Bo was the first Bichon Miscellaneous Class winner in the East. Champion Camelot's Brassy Nickel CD, CDX, bred, owned and trained by Pam Goldman, winner of the 1984 national specialty, became the only national specialty Best of Breed winner to become an obedience titlist. The first Bichon to earn an Obedience Trial Championship, or OTCh, was Ch. C. & D.'s Watson UD, owned and trained by Billijo Porter. Chanel XVII, owned and trained by Shirley Bisignano, became the first Bichon to win a *Dog World* award for earning all three obedience titles in less than one year. In the 20 years since AKC recognition, Bichons have earned 224 CDs, 54 CDXs, and 15 UDs. There has also been at least one Bichon to earn a tracking title, and one champion who competed in weight pulling contests along with her Malamute housemates.

The Bichon's clownish nature often appears in the obedience ring. They love applause and laughter. My own Ch. Camelot's Brassy Nickel CD, CDX would stop and stack in a show pose whenever he heard applause. This was

Ch. Sea Star's Sandpiper practicing heeling. Owned and trained by Billie Jo Porter, El Paso, Texas.

OTCh. C. and D.'s B.A. Watson, UD is the first Bichon to earn the title of Obedience Trial Champion; place in a Gaines event, which he accomplished in Open; earn the *Dog World* Award; be ranked in the obedience systems in Group, ranking fifth in Non-Sporting under the Delaney System; and win high in trial 22 times, an all-time record for Bichons in obedience. Watson was bred by Dolores Wolske, is by Ch. C.and D.'s Freedom Call ex Ch. C. and D.'s Bit of Spring. His owner and trainer is Billie Jo Porter of El Paso, Texas.

probably as a result of his specials career when he won many groups and Bests in Show. In the obedience ring, he would look at me as if to say, "Are you sure you're talking to me? I don't think I know you." Spectators would laugh, Nicky would wag his tail and I'd feel silly. Bichons are very good at making their owners feel foolish.

It has been said, by some who do not know the breed, that Bichons are not smart and are difficult to train. Those of us who train in obedience are well aware of the enormous intelligence of the breed. There is in this breed an ability to play dumb. If a Bichon decides that it doesn't want to cooperate, it may plant itself on the ground and refuse to move or, more likely, clown around and go for the laugh that is sure to come, especially in the ring! If obedience judges could make house calls, there would probably be many more titlists as well as OTChs!

The standard says "A cheerful attitude is the hallmark of this breed and one should settle for nothing less." Any training method that makes the dog appear unhappy must not be used. Because Bichons are such a happy breed, always willing to please, training sessions must be fun. They do not train

Bunnyrun Little Deuce Coupe, CDX taking first place Veteran (non-regular obedience class) at Orlando, Florida in 1990. Helen Temmel, owner-handler.

easily with the old military methods, because they are capable of reasoning! One must first show a Bichon what the exercise is all about, and then gently lead him through it, teaching each part separately. Though this may sound difficult and time-consuming, it is really the most efficient method for getting the best results. This is a sensitive, intelligent dog that responds best to praise and affection. Food rewards may be useful in motivating a dog that is having difficulty in understanding the trainer's requests.

BASIC OBEDIENCE FOR PUPPIES

Obedience training begins in the litter, as the puppy learns discipline from both its mother and breeder. By the time the puppy goes to its new home, it should be well socialized to both people and dogs, and should be accustomed to a crate for travel and for sleeping and eating. The crate is a new puppy's best friend, for it prevents him from dirtying the floor and from getting into mischief or worse in the absence of his owner. There are many books and articles on the subject of crate training that are available to the novice dog owner.

Good house manners are the result of good puppy training. Puppies are creatures of habit and learn by repetition, so preventing bad habits while

Ch. Sea Star's Sandpiper, making a good Group placement. Bred by Jill Cohen and Jean Campbell, "Piper" belongs to Billie Jo Porter of El Paso, Texas. Billie Jo trains and handles her own dogs in the obedience ring.

Top left: *OTCh C. and D.'s B.A. Watson, UD* doing a glove exercise (Directed Retrieve), in Utility. "Watson," owned and trained by Billie Jo Porter of El Paso, Texas. Center: *Ch. Sea Star's Sandpiper* retrieving a toy during obedience training. Lower left: Receiving instructions for a directed return in Utility, *OTCh. C. and D.'s B.A. Watson, UD* with his owner/trainer Billie Jo Porter.

fostering good ones is the only way to train. Positive attention gets positive results. Just like little children, puppies look for attention any way they can, and just like little children, if they can't get positive attention, they will do something that gets them negative attention. Ignoring negative behaviors, not even rewarding them with any words, is the fastest way to get rid of those behaviors. Bichons will do everything for lavish praise and love. Bichons live for the love and approval of

their humans. This is the best motivation.

Dog owners need their dogs to behave well both at home and in public. Dogs should not jump up on people or furniture without permission. Preventing this behavior from the time of the puppy's arrival in the new home is the best training. Never allow the puppy on the furniture. Keep a buckle collar and leash on the puppy. If he

starts to jump up, give the leash a good, hard yank and say, **"NO!"** in a very firm tone of voice. He wants approval, so when he is on the floor, praise him generously.

Housebreaking (with a crate) is best done on a schedule that is suited to the family's life. Everyone in the household must be consistent so that the puppy does not become confused. If a Bichon is raised by its breeder in a clean environment, housebreaking will not be too difficult. It cannot be stressed enough that the crate is the best piece of equipment that both the owner and the dog can have. If done with a crate and a schedule, housebreaking can be accomplished in a very short time, provided that the puppy is not too young. The optimum time for acquiring and training a new puppy is between ten and 12 weeks.

Don't wait until the puppy is six months old to begin training it to walk on leash, come when called, sit, and lie down. You will have wasted the best weeks for teaching, because we now know that what a puppy learns in the first 16 weeks of life stay with it better than what it learns after that time. This is not to say that a dog will not learn after 16 weeks. It

Four Paws Wee-Wee pads are scientifically treated to attract puppies when nature calls. The plastic lining prevents damage to floors and carpets. Photo courtesy of Four Paws.

means that what a dog learns early in life it will remember more strongly and that training will be easier for the dog to remember and obey.

In today's society, all dogs must be kept on a

Directed jumping done by *Ch. Sea Star's Sandpiper* being owner-trained by Billie Jo Porter, El Paso, Texas.

leash, for their own safety, and in some places, by law. No one likes to be pulled down the street by a dog. Even a little dog is capable of exerting an enormous amount of force. Small puppies can learn to walk nicely on lead in a very short time. In the beginning, the puppy takes the owner, but after a few days, the owner can just change direction without saying a word, praising the puppy when it catches up. Before long, it will learn to pay attention and stay at the owner's side. Older dogs will need a leash correction, a quick pop back with the leash while saying "No pull." When teaching a puppy to walk on leash, don't say "Come on!"—this will cause confusion when the "come" exercise is being taught. It is better to say "Let's go," or more formally "Heel," when the puppy is to do precise heeling. Formal training for the competition ring can begin when the puppy is four or five months old and knows how to walk on lead, sit, and come when called.

To teach the heel exercise, have the puppy, wearing its buckle collar and leash, sit at your left side. Hold the leash and the seam of your pants with your right hand and pull the dog as close to you as possible. Say "Heel" and step forward on your left foot. The dog has no choice but to go with you in the correct position. When the dog begins to move, praise it lavishly. Make right turns, left turns and right about turns. Zigzag, change directions. Don't let the dog and you get bored! Always keep the dog off balance so that it will have to pay attention. If it pays attention, it will hear and obey commands. There is a difference between formal heeling and walking nicely with the owner. When there is no need to have the dog close to the left side, you can use the command

Helen Temmel of Dunedin, Florida with her Bichon, *Bunnyrun Little Deuce Coupe, CDX* and Bunny's Papillon friend.

OTCh. C. and D.'s B.A. Watson, UD proving his agility in the tire jump exercise. Owned and trained by Billie Jo Porter, El Paso, Texas.

"Let's go!" together with the "No pull" command for controlled walking. Release the dog from any exercise by saying "OK!" and praising.

Coming when called is, next to housebreaking, the most important skill a puppy must have. Most dogs are returned, given away, abandoned or taken to shelters because they have not been taught this skill by their owners. A dog comes when it is called only if it is praised and loved when it does so. Never call a dog to punish it. Always go to the dog if discipline is necessary.

Never call a dog more than once. It will learn to wait for the third or fourth call before coming. If the dog does not come when you call it, walk slowly toward it smiling, and, holding the collar, back up to the spot from which you called it. Praise, release, put the leash on. Facing the dog at the end of the leash, call, "Rover, come!" and pop back on the leash. When the dog starts moving, gather in the leash and praise the dog when it reaches you. Repeat until the dog begins to move before the leash is popped. When the dog is coming without the leash pop, it's time to start moving backward a few steps, with the leash on. Once the puppy is coming when called, back up as it moves toward you, gathering in the leash. Gradually increase the distance until the pup will come to you from anywhere in the room. Then try calling from another room. Always remember to praise the pup when it reaches you. This is another place where food rewards are very helpful.

Teaching a puppy to sit requires a lot of patience. There are several methods that work well. One is to hold a treat at the level of the puppy's nose and to lift it straight up over the pup's head, saying "Sit" while guiding the rear end

toward the ground. As soon as the puppy sits, it gets the treat. Another is to lift straight up with the leash, front feet staying on the floor, and hold until the puppy sits. Praise and reward with a treat as soon as its bottom hits the floor. As with all other exercises, repetition and consistency are the keys to success. Always praise the puppy when it has done what is required.

The down is probably the most difficult exercise for a novice trainer to teach a puppy. This is because lying down on command is an act of submission. All dogs would rather lie down than stand or sit, but when *they* want to do it. To be made to lie down is a submissive behavior that

The agility dog walk. OTCh. C. and D.'s B.A. Watson, UD is owned and trained by Billie Jo Porter, El Paso, Texas.

Right over the top of a six-foot high frame! *Ch. C. and D.'s B.A. Watson, UD* scores again in agility for his owner/trainer Billie Jo Porter of El Paso, Texas.

must be gently taught. To teach your Bichon to lie down on command, put on its collar and leash and have it sit. Kneel beside the dog, on its right, and put your left hand on its withers. Say "Down," and take its front feet in your right hand and slide them forward while gently pushing down your left hand. When it is all the way down, praise lavishly, saying, "Good down!" When the dog begins to go down on its own, point to the floor with your right hand as a signal each time you say"Down!" When walking the dog, you can drop to your left knee, sliding your left hand down the leash to the collar, and holding it on the ground until the dog goes down. Then, praise and release, saying, "OK!" Do NOT use the word "down" to mean "get off the furniture." You will confuse your puppy. Making your puppy do a sit or a down before it can eat, go for a walk or a ride in the car will hasten its learning of these commands. A dog that earns its rewards by obeying commands will remember its training.

Other useful commands your Bichon should learn are, "Hop in," for going into the crate, the car or other opening that the trainer wants; "Stay," meaning "Don't move!" in the sit or down position; "Wait," meaning "it won't be long";

OTCh. C. and D.'s B.A. Watson, UD again proves his outstanding agility as he makes his way through a collapsed tunnel. Billie Jo Porter is the owner/trainer of this exciting little Bichon.

and "Off," meaning "get off the furniture, my lap, etc."

It is worth repeating that dogs are creatures of habit and learn by repetition. Therefore, it is important to teach only those habits that are wanted and not those that are undesirable. If a puppy is teased and grabbed at, it will learn to bite to protect itself. Children and adults must be aware of their own behavior around puppies and dogs so they do not provoke bad behavior. All any dog wants is a loving home, a warm bed, and a friend to call his own.

The flying Bichon! OTCh. C. and D.'s B.A. Watson, UD clearing a spread jump in agility. Watson is proudly owned and trained by Billie Jo Porter of El Paso, Texas.

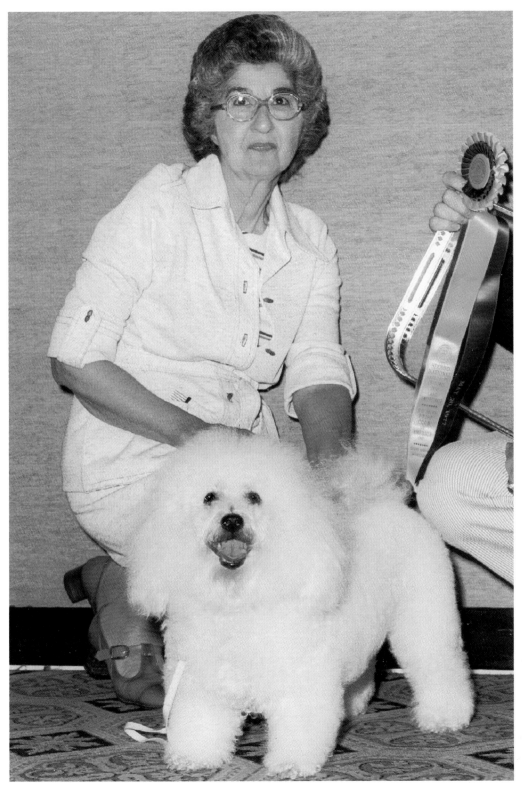

Mrs. Helen D. Temmel with *Ch. Sandra de la Lande de Belleville, UD, Bermuda CD*, a well-known and sucessful winner of the late 1970s.

Bichon Rescue

It is a sad fact of life, and a heartbreaking one to those who love dogs, that occasions do arise when even the most delightful of canines fall into unscrupulous hands, thus becoming the objects of neglect, cruelty, or both. The fancy has become increasingly concerned over these incidents to the point that many people and many clubs are taking steps toward helping these victims, whose efforts and the results we applaud.

The Bichon Frise Club of America is both concerned and taking action. We gladly share information with our readers to encourage support and cooperation with the Bichon Frise Rescue Squad.

Bichon Frise Rescue, in conjunction with the national specialty club, became active around

Ch. Glen Elfred's Mr. Chips, ROM was acquired by Eleanor Grassick of Elmont, New York at three-and-a-half years of age after having been badly beaten from head to tail. The Grassicks nursed him back to health and taught him to show on a show lead. His first-time out he won a four-point major owner/handled. He became the sire of 14 champions and a CD.

BEST OF BREED OR VARIETY
CENTRAL NEW YORK KENNEL CLUB
KLEIN   NOV 12 77

JANESVILLE-BELOIT
KENNEL CLUB
MAY 3 1986
NON
SPORTING
GROUP
K BOOTH
PHOTO

NON SPORTING

1990. Approximately 30 rescue workers are now participants across the country. Their efforts are coordinated by Laura Fox, a Bichon fancier and owner of some outstanding Bichons, including one with multiple Best in Show and Group victories to his credit. Laura Fox has herself personally rescued and placed over 50 Bichons since formation of this work.

Workers for Bichon Rescue all operate under the same rules and regulations. All use the same adoption and release forms, and have centralized most of their rescue efforts. All keep track of who has an overabundance of rescue dogs and of who has room for more.

Laura has prepared a "how-to" brochure, a rescue list of active members, and the adoption

Ch. Scamper Gatlock of Druid owned and bred by Betty Keatley, Betsy Schley, and Laura Fox-Meachen. Scamper was in the top ten Bichons in 1983 and 1984.

and release forms. She has also written a job description for the rescue chairperson, which position she now holds, "but certainly not forever."

THE BICHON RESCUE LIST

As a suggestion to folks looking for a lovely Bichon as a family companion, contact the National Hotline for Bichon Frise Rescue, Laura Fox (414) 878-4446. All those I've met or heard about who have done this have been extremely happy with the results, and dearly love their rescue dog or dogs.

Take, for example, Jac (whose name stands for *Joliet Animal Control*), who had been found wandering the streets of Joliet, Illinois, by the Animal Welfare. He was held for seven days and then scheduled for euthanization. However, Animal Welfare cared! They found Laura Fox's name and address in the *Project Breed* book and called to see if she could come pick him up. Of course she could and she did. Jac looked a bit "scuzzy" to her, so she took him to her vet, who found that the dog had eaten rat poison and was hemorrhaging. The vet immediately put him on vitamin K. Other than that he checked out healthy.

Taking him home that night, Laura noticed a large lump on his side, very similar to an umbilical hernia but protruding from his right side. So she returned him to the vet, who held him for three days and then opened him up to find the problem. It was a large puncture wound that entered the muscle tissue and left a gaping hole that allowed the muscle to protrude through. The entry wound had all the earmarks of having been done by a knife.

The happy part of the story is now being enjoyed by Jac. He came through the surgery with flying colors and now lives with his new "Mommy," also a rescue person, Phillis Peppard. Laura tells us "Jac smiles, Jac waves, and Jac loves the world." Also Jac reminds Phillis and Laura every day that every Bichon deserves a chance to have a good life.

Should you ever be called upon to rescue a Bichon, here are the ground rules on how it is done.

HOW TO RESCUE A BICHON

The following is a guideline for rescuing a Bichon Frise. These are recommendations only, but they have been developed through many years of experience. Feel free to offer comments or to suggest modifications to these guidelines.

HOW TO RESCUE A BICHON

I. Preparing for Your Role in Rescuing Bichons
    A. Preparations for housing extra dogs
        1. You need a place to isolate incoming dogs on a short-term basis.
        2. Identify veterinarians in your area
            a. check prices on vet care
            b. know the vets' hours and their policies on emergency care
    B. Preparing your dogs for incoming rescue dogs
        1. Inoculate for kennel cough, rabies, and make sure they have all booster shots
        2. If possible, have a standby housing plan for either your puppies or the rescue dog
    C. Contact people in the local Bichon club and ask for assistance in housing and placing.
    D. Contact the humane societies, vets or other potential rescue sources in your local area,   and let them know who you are and what you're willing to do
    E. Get and photocopy copies of the custodial adoptions agreement and the transfer of ownership, and have them ready for use.
II. Rescuing Bichons
    A. What to do when you're contacted about taking in a rescue Bichon
        1. Accept the dog, but on your terms, not theirs
            a. never pay for a rescue dog
            b. make people sign the release form or refuse to take the dog (remember the release form is going to protect you against litigation)
            c. if possible, get AKC papers signed over to you
            d. get health records, name and phone number of former vet
            e. call vet and check on recent inoculations check out personality of dog and owner find out about health problems
        2. Take the dog immediately to a vet
    B. Housing of the rescue dog
        1. Keep the rescue dogs away from your dogs
            a. don't let the rescue dog go to the bathroom where your dogs go
        2. Keep the dog two to three weeks at least
            a. place it in various situations to best test its reactions to people and habitat
            b. *don't place a dog that's vicious.* Don't place a dog that bites you or your family. Unfortunately you may have to make the decision to have this dog put to sleep.
        3. Get the dog neutered or the bitch spayed.
        4. Take a picture of the dog and start a file
            a. keep all records of monies paid out for vet costs
    C. Placing the dog
        1. The interviewing process for finding a good home
            a. have at least two interviews
            b. try to match the dog to a compatible family
            c. don't place a dog with a family with children under the age of four
            d. try to place the dog with a family with a fenced-in yard
        2. When you adopt the dog out remember to use adoptions forms to protect yourself
        3. Do not release AKC papers; hold in dog's file
        4. Do not give out former owner's name
        5. Ask for a donation
        6. Make sure the new owners know they can bring the dog back if they are not happy with it
    D. Follow-up
        1. Check up on the dog after placing it.

A Tribute to Roy Copelin

Roy Copelin was a dedicated fancier of the Bichon Frise in the United States. Roy had enviable talent for understanding and appreciating all the attributes which make these little dogs unique and beautiful. He was truly a person with a reliable "eye for a dog," judging by the quality of the Bichons he bred and owned. Roy's dogs have type, soundness, quality and personality, adding up to the quintessential character that makes a Bichon a Bichon. The import, Ch. Montravia Jazz M'Tazz, won many admirers in a short time and became a ROM Producer and sire of other important winners for Roy's program. Ch. Chez Mar China Doll or "China" also became an important name in the dog world. And "Goose"—formally Ch. Sumarco Alaafee Top Gun—became the most famous of all Roy's dogs. Unfortunately, Goose's first Best in Show was after Roy's death and he did not have the chance to enjoy that auspicious occasion. Goose also became an ROM Producer and top sire.

Devoted as he was to his dogs, Roy left his dogs in the good hands of his close friend Ellen Roberts. With the dogs, he left a detailed description of the breeding plans for their descendants: today this plan is being carried out to the letter and with great success.

EDITOR'S NOTE: *The Editor wishes to thank Miss Nicholas for researching Mr. Copelin's contribution to the Bichon world. In Mr. Copelin's final days, he was working on a Bichon Frise book for T.F.H. Publications. Unfortunately he didn't live to complete the entire book, and his computer files of the completed chapters were inaccessible to his family. While we do not have Mr. Copelin's words to share with our readers, we do have his beautiful dogs.*
—Andrew De Prisco

Roy Copelin's top three Bichons: Jazz, China and Goose exemplifying the excellent type and quality of Mr. Copelin's breeding program. Each of these tremendously important dogs continues to make an impact on the breed through its progeny. Photograph courtesy of Ellen Roberts.

Index

Page numbers in **boldface** refer to illustrations.

SUGGESTED READING

H-1091, 912 pp
over 1100 color photos

TS-175, 896 pp
over 1300 color photos

TW-136, 256 pp
over 200 color photos

TS-204, 160 pp
over 50 line drawings

TS-205, 156 pp
over 130 color photos

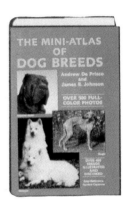

H-1106, 912 pp
over 400 color photos

TS-212, 256 pp
over 140 color photos

TS-220, 64 pp
over 50 color illus.

SUGGESTED READING

PS-872, 240 pp
178 color illus.

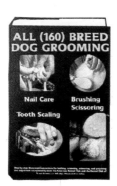

H-1095, 272 pp
Over 160 color illus

KW-227, 96 pp
100 color photos

H-1016, 254 pp
135 photos

TS-130, 160 pp
50 color illus.

TS-264, 192 pp
over 300 color photos

TW-113, 256 pp
200 color photos

TS-249, 224 pp
300 color photos

TS-258, 160 pp
Over 200 color photos

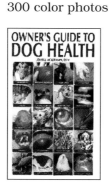

TS-214, 432 pp
over 300 color photos

CHOOSING A DOG FOR LIFE

TS-257, 384 pp
over 700 color photos